I0559472

"Timothy Brady's *Reading Greek with the Desert Fathers: An Intermediate Greek Reader* is a wonderful way to build your Greek reading skills while also learning more about a fascinating period of church history."

Robert L. Plummer, Ph.D.
Founder, Daily Dose of Greek
Collin and Evelyn Aikman Professor of Biblical Studies
The Southern Baptist Theological Seminary

"*Reading Greek with the Desert Fathers* by Timothy Brady offers a great resource for extensive reading of Greek at the intermediate level. Brady's adapted text promotes reading fluency in New Testament Greek while providing a unique entry point for reading the Desert Fathers."

Jennifer Noonan, Ph.D.
Instructor of Old Testament and Women's Leadership
Columbia International University

"This book is a Greek Teacher's dream. Not only is the Greek modified to perfectly serve biblical Greek students, the selected texts are both interesting and spiritually instructive. I can confidently hand this to students who have finished first year Greek and know that the resource will help them expand their facility in the Biblical language."

Timothy E. Miller, Ph.D.
VP of Academics, Dean of Faculty
Shepherds Theological Seminary

Reading Greek with the Desert Fathers

An Intermediate Greek Reader

Timothy Brady

SOJOURNER
PRESS

Unless otherwise indicated, all Scripture quotations are taken from the New King James Version. Copyright © by Thomas Nelson, Inc. 1982. All rights reserved.

Cover design by Hunter Hays

For bulk, special sales, or ministry purchases, please contact us at sales@sojournerpress.org.

Reading Greek with the Desert Fathers:
An Intermediate Greek Reader
Copyright © 2024 by Timothy Brady
Published by Sojourner Press
Raleigh, NC, 27603
sojournerpress.org

Trade paperback ISBN: 978-1-960255-12-9
ePub ISBN: 978-1-960255-13-6

Printed in the United States of America

Contents

English Translations

Preface

In ancient times, Greek-speaking schoolboys were taught to read and write by modeling their own compositions after the greatest examples of literature and rhetoric. One of the most basic tools at their disposal was the teacher's *paraphrasis* or "paraphrase."[1] The schoolmaster would take a difficult text and reformulate it, breaking down the syntax into bite-sized sentences and replacing obscure vocabulary with everyday words. That way, the students could meaningfully engage with advanced content, while still learning at their own pace. These graded Greek readers began as early as the first century BC and persisted all throughout antiquity and into the Byzantine era.[2]

Nowadays, the field of second language acquisition has shown that extensive reading in the target language confers a host of benefits: incidental acquisition of vocabulary and grammar, ease of language processing, increased fluency, and heightened motivation.[3] However, these benefits only accrue if the learners

---

1 Theon, *Progymnasmata* 1.14, ed. Leonard Spengel vol. 2 (Leipzig: Teubner, 1854), 57–130. Cf. also Maria Ypsilanti and Laura Franco, *Nonnus' Paraphrase between Poetry, Rhetoric, and Theology: Rewriting the Fourth Gospel in the Fifth Century*, Mnemosyne, Supplements, Late Antique Literature 436 (Leiden: Koninklijke Brill NV, 2021), 39–40. There is also evidence of students writing out similar paraphrases.

2 Matthew Roberts, *Biblical Epic and Rhetorical Paraphrase in Late Antiquity* (Liverpool: Francis Cairns, 1985), 44.

3 Paul Nation, "The Language Learning Benefits of Extensive Reading," *The Language Teacher* 21, no. 5 (1997): 13–16.

are consuming large amounts of material that is "at their level."

It turns out that a very effective way of ensuring that the reading is "at their level" is to control the vocabulary, while still keeping the text rich in grammatical features. In fact, vocabulary level is such a strong predictor of overall comprehension that even if students are unfamiliar with some of the grammatical forms, they can still usually piece together the meaning quite well as long as they know enough of the individual words.[4] This in turn keeps motivation high, reinforces passive familiarity with grammatical structures, and introduces new vocabulary at regular intervals and in varied settings. So what is needed is a wealth of texts simple enough for students to read on their own and compelling enough to hold their interest.[5]

That is where this graded reader comes in. It contains authentic texts from antiquity, which have been adapted for students of New Testament Greek. Any words in the original that do not appear in the New Testament have been substituted with their appropriate equivalents. The grammar has likewise been

---

[4] George Klare, "Assessing Readability," *Reading Research Quarterly* 10, no. 1 (1974–1975): 62–102; Paul Nation, "Vocabulary size, growth and use," *The Bilingual Lexicon* (Philadelphia: John Benjamins, 1993): 115–134.

[5] While the only statistics available are from modern language programs, the research still suggests that this kind of content should be consumed on the order of hundreds of thousands of running words per year (Paul Nation, "Planning and Running an Extensive Reading Program," *NUCB Journal of Language Culture and Communication* 3, no. 1 (2001): 1–8).

harmonized to the New Testament. Moreover, instead of drawing vocabulary indiscriminately from the 5,594 lemmas in the New Testament, this reader restricts itself to only the 294 words that occur 50 times or more. This short list covers 80% of the text of the New Testament and forms the core of many beginner Greek courses (such as for instance William Mounce's *Basics of Biblical Greek*). This paraphrase is designed to be easy enough so that even someone with only a basic grasp of the grammar can still understand enough to benefit from it. That means that any student with a starter vocabulary of under three hundred words should be able to dive right in.[6]

This paraphrase has been checked over by many hands for accuracy and fidelity. The original text has been simplified enough for the content to be captured in idiomatic Greek, within the confines of the core vocabulary and without compromising authenticity and proper usage. Every clause has been thoroughly corrected against actual Koine literature to ensure that what students read here is preparing them for unsimplified Greek later on.[7] Wherever the core vocabulary

---

6 Koine Greek is well-adapted to vocabulary curating of this kind. While equipped with an enormous total lexical stock of rare and technical words, it has a working core vocabulary less than half the size of Latin or English. That means that common words in Greek are recycled far more readily than in other languages (Wilfred Major, "It's Not the Size, It's the Frequency: The Value of Using a Core Vocabulary in Beginning and Intermediate Greek," *CPL Online* 4, no. 1 (2008): 1–24.

7 The Greek of this edition is intentionally modeled after the style of John. John relies on parataxis, concrete imagery, repetition, and a paucity of particles and literary flourishes—all features which combine to make the Johannine corpus easily the most accessible texts of the New

of 294 words has proved insufficient, a less common New Testament term has been substituted in its place, underlined, and glossed at the bottom of the page.[8] In some cases, the content has been modified slightly or a conceptual equivalent has been supplied instead for clarity or naturalness of expression. If the reader is interested, the original Greek texts are available at sojournerpress.org/desertfathers for comparison.

Like the *paraphrasis* of old, this reader brings classic literature within reach of the novice. We hope that by providing edifying works from the early church at the beginners' level, we will enable them to practice their Greek while exploring their Christian heritage at the same time. The focus here is not so much parsing forms, memorizing vocabulary lists, and writing out translations (as important as these skills are), but rather gaining facility and practical experience with the language. We want to give weary Greek students

---

Testament. And yet, even John has a vocabulary of over 1,000 lexical items, putting him out of reach of true beginners. This graded reader simulates the earthy, everyday Koine of the fourth Gospel, with a streamlined vocabulary.

8   These glosses have been added sparingly. Studies in second language acquisition suggest that to maximize comprehension and vocabulary building, 95–98% of the text should consist of known words (Marcella Hu Hsueh-chao and Paul Nation, "Unknown Vocabulary Density and Reading Comprehension," *Reading in a Foreign Language* 13, no. 1 [2000]: 403–30). Any more than that, and the text is too easy; students will be starved for new vocabulary (and probably bored). Any fewer than that, however, and students struggle with comprehension and lose the ability to guess at words from the context. Moreover, a text cluttered with definitions and explanatory notes is more intimidating and difficult to read. So in this edition, the words outside the core vocabulary never exceed 2–5% of the total text.

a break from studying paradigms and a chance to try out their hard-won skills on live texts. And ultimately, this is meant to be one more stepping stone to studying the word of God in its original language.

Greek Texts

The stories in this section are authentic documents written in Koine Greek. The grammar and vocabulary have been harmonized to the style of the New Testament, and glosses have been added for more difficult vocabulary.

Introduction

This volume is a selection of the readings from the Desert Fathers. These were the first generation of Christian monks, who settled in the Egyptian wilderness in the fourth century AD. These men fled the urban centers of the Roman Empire, where Christianity was rapidly becoming vogue, in obedience to what they felt was Christ's command to them: *If you want to be perfect, go, sell what you have and give to the poor, and you will have treasure in heaven; and come, follow Me* (Matt 19:21). The record of their exploits was compiled in Greek probably between the fifth and sixth centuries, but much of the material stretches back to the very beginnings of the movement.[1] Students of the Desert Fathers will often find some aspects of their faith compelling, while others will seem foreign or even off-putting, but a humble heart will discover much edification and wisdom in the record of their words and deeds.

---

[1] The Alphabetical Collection is taken from the Patrologia Graeca (PG 65:71–440), while the Anonymous Collection is from the critical text of John Wortley, *An Introduction to the Desert Fathers* (Cambridge: Cambridge University Press, 2019).

1. How to Pray

Προσῆλθέ τις τῶν ἀδελφῶν τινὶ πρεσβυτέρῳ μένοντι ἐν τῷ Σινᾷ ὄρει καὶ παρεκάλεσεν αὐτὸν λέγων· "πάτερ, εἰπέ μοι πῶς δεῖ με προσεύχεσθαι· πολλὰς γὰρ ἔχω ἁμαρτίας ἐνώπιον τοῦ Θεοῦ." λέγει αὐτῷ ὁ πρεσβύτερος· "ἐγώ, τέκνον, ὅταν προσεύχωμαι, οὕτως λέγω· Κύριε, θέλω <u>δουλεῦσαί</u>² σοι καθὼς <u>ἐδούλευσα</u> τῷ Σατανᾷ, καὶ ἀγαπῆσαί σε καθὼς ἠγάπησα τὴν ἁμαρτίαν."

2. The Watchful Father

Ἤμεθά ποτε ἐν Ῥαϊθοῦ καὶ ἔλεγον ἡμῖν οἱ ἀδελφοὶ ὅτι ἦν τις πρεσβύτερος μέγας καθήμενος ἐν τῷ ὄρει τῆς γῆς Ἰσραήλ. καὶ οὕτως ἐτήρει ὁ πρεσβύτερος οὗτος τὸ ἑαυτοῦ πνεῦμα, ὥστε μηδὲ περιπατεῖν αὐτὸν εἰ μὴ πρῶτον προσηύξατο. καὶ τότε πορευθεὶς ὀλίγον καὶ <u>στὰς</u>³, πάλιν προσηύχετο καὶ <u>ἐδοκίμαζεν</u>⁴ ἑαυτὸν λέγων· "πῶς ἔχομεν ἀδελφέ; τί ποιεῖς;" καὶ εἰ μὲν εὕρισκε τὸ πνεῦμα αὐτοῦ δοξάζον τὸν Θεὸν ἢ προσευχόμενον, καλῶς· εἰ δὲ εὕρισκεν ἑαυτὸν ἄλλο τι ποιοῦντα, εὐθὺς <u>ἐπετίμησεν</u>⁵ ἑαυτῷ λέγων· "ἐλθὲ

---

2 δουλεύω, 'I serve'

3 στάς 'having stood (still); stopped' (masc. sing. aor. part. ἵστημι 'I stand')

4 δοκιμάζω 'I test; examine'

5 ἐπιτιμάω 'I rebuke'

ὧδε, μωρέ¹, πάλιν εἰς τὸ ἔργον σου." καὶ τοῦτο ἐπὶ
πολὺ ἐποίει ὅπου ἂν περιεπάτει. καὶ ἔλεγεν πρὸς
ἑαυτὸν καθ' ἡμέραν ὁ πρεσβύτερος· "ἀδελφέ, ἐγγὺς²
ἡ ὥρα τοῦ ἀπελθεῖν καὶ οὐκ ἐποίησας οὐδέν." τούτῳ
ποτὲ προσῆλθεν ὁ Σατανᾶς καὶ λέγει αὐτῷ· "τί ἔτι
ἐργάζῃ³; οὐ γὰρ ἔστιν ἐλπὶς τοῦ σῴζεσθαί σε." λέγει
αὐτῷ καὶ αὐτός· "καὶ ἐὰν μὴ σωθῶ ἐγώ, πάντως⁴ ἐπὶ
τῆς κεφαλῆς σου εὑρίσκομαι ἱστάμενος, καὶ σὺ δὲ
ἔσχατος πάντων ἐν Γεέννῃ."

3. The Fallen Pillar

*Abba Anthony of the Desert (c. 250–356) was the most
famous of the Desert Fathers. This story illustrates the
often neglected distinction between spiritual gifts and
true holiness.*

Ἤκουσεν ὁ ἀββᾶς Ἀντώνιος περί τινος ἄλλου
πατρός, ποιήσαντος σημεῖον ἐν τῇ ὁδῷ· εἶδεν
γὰρ πρεσβυτέρους τινάς πολὺν χρόνον ἤδη
πορευομένους ἐν τῇ ὁδῷ καὶ μὴ δυναμένους ἔτι
πορευθῆναι. καὶ ἐλάλησεν τοῖς θηρίοις⁵ καὶ εἶπεν
αὐτοῖς ἵνα ἐνέγκωσι⁶ τοὺς πρεσβυτέρους ἕως οὗ

---

1 μωρός, -όν, -ά 'fool'

2 ἐγγύς, -ύ 'near'

3 ἐργάζομαι 'I work'

4 πάντως 'certainly; nevertheless'

5 θηρίον, -ου, τό 'wild beast; animal'

6 ἐνέγκωσι 'that they should carry' (3 per. plur. aor. subj. φέρω 'I carry')

ἔλθωσι πρὸς Ἀντώνιον. οἱ οὖν πρεσβύτεροι εἶπον τῷ
ἀββᾷ Ἀντωνίῳ ταῦτα. καὶ λέγει αὐτοῖς· "δοκεῖ μοι
ὁ πατὴρ οὗτος πλοῖον εἶναι πολλὰ ἔχον ἀγαθά· οὐκ
οἶδα δὲ εἰ <u>ἐλεύσεται</u>[7] ἐν εἰρήνῃ εἰς τὸν <u>λιμένα</u>[8]." καὶ
μετὰ χρόνον ἄρχεται <u>ἐξαίφνης</u>[9] ὁ ἀββᾶς Ἀντώνιος
<u>κλαίειν</u>[10] καὶ κράζειν ἐν φωνῇ μεγάλῃ. λέγουσιν
αὐτῷ οἱ μαθηταὶ αὐτοῦ· "τί <u>κλαίεις</u>, ἀββᾶ;" καὶ εἶπεν
ὁ πρεσβύτερος· "μέγας <u>στῦλος</u>[11] τῆς ἐκκλησίας
νῦν ἔπεσεν (ἔλεγε δὲ περὶ τοῦ ἄλλου πατρός)·
ἀλλὰ ἀπέλθετε," φησίν, "πρὸς αὐτὸν καὶ βλέπετε
τὸ <u>γεγονός</u>[12]." ἀπέρχονται οὖν οἱ μαθηταί, καὶ
εὑρίσκουσι τὸν πατέρα ἐπὶ τῆς γῆς καθήμενον, καὶ
<u>κλαίοντα</u> τὴν ἁμαρτίαν ἣν ἐποίησεν. ἰδὼν δὲ τοὺς
μαθητὰς τοῦ ἀββᾶ Ἀντωνίου, λέγει· "εἴπατε τῷ πατρὶ
ὅτι· 'πάτερ, παρακάλεσον τὸν Θεὸν ὑπὲρ ἐμοῦ, ἵνα
δώσῃ μοι ἑπτὰ μόνας ἡμέρας, ἵνα <u>μετανοήσω</u>[13].'" ἀλλὰ
μεθ' ἡμέρας μόνον τρεῖς, ἀπέθανεν.

---

7 ἐλεύσεται 'it will arrive' (3 per. sing. fut. ἔρχομαι 'I come')

8 λιμήν, λιμένος, ὁ 'harbor, port'

9 ἐξαίφνης 'suddenly'

10 κλαίω 'I weep; weep for, mourn'

11 στῦλος, -ου, ὁ 'pillar'

12 τὸ γεγονός 'what has happened' (neut. sing. perf. part. γίνομαι 'I become, happen')

13 μετανοέω 'I repent'

4. The Right Answer

Humility was as important to the fathers as spiritual acuity, and the very wise are often portrayed as equally discrete.

Προσῆλθόν ποτε πατέρες τῷ ἀββᾷ Ἀντωνίῳ, καὶ ἦν ὁ ἀββᾶς Ἰωσὴφ μετ' αὐτῶν. καὶ θέλων ὁ πρεσβύτερος <u>πειράσαι</u>[1] αὐτούς, ἠρώτησεν περὶ ῥήματός τινος <u>δυσκόλου</u>[2] ἐκ τῆς γραφῆς. καὶ ἤρξατο ἐρωτᾷν αὐτοὺς ἀπὸ τῶν ἐσχάτων ἕως τῶν μεγάλων λέγων· "τί ἐστι τὸ ῥῆμα τοῦτο; τί θέλει τοῦτο λέγειν;" καὶ ἕκαστος ἀπεκρίνατο κατὰ τὴν ἰδίαν δύναμιν. ὁ δὲ ἀββᾶς Ἀντώνιος ἑκάστῳ ἔλεγεν· "<u>οὔπω</u>[3] εὗρες· τοῦτο οὐ καλῶς εἶπας." τότε ἐσχάτῳ πάντων λέγει τῷ ἀββᾷ Ἰωσήφ· "σὺ πῶς λέγεις εἶναι τὸν λόγον τοῦτον;" ὁ δὲ ἀποκρίνεται· "οὐκ οἶδα." λέγει οὖν ὁ ἀββᾶς Ἀντώνιος· "ἀλλὰ ἀββᾶς Ἰωσὴφ εὗρε τὴν ὁδόν, ὅτι εἶπεν· 'οὐκ οἶδα.'"

---

1 πειράζω 'I test; tempt'

2 δύσκολος 'difficult; hard'

3 οὔπω 'not yet'

5. Steal the Donkey

The desert community of Scetis was one of the great centers of monastic life. Younger members of the brotherhood would often venture deeper into the wilderness in search of hermits and the wisdom they had to offer.

Ἀδελφοὶ προσῆλθον τῷ ἀββᾷ Ἀντωνίῳ ἀπὸ Σκήτεως. καὶ καταβάντες πρὸς τὴν θάλασσαν πορευθῆναι πρὸς αὐτόν, εὗρον πρεσβύτερον θέλοντα καὶ αὐτὸν ἀπελθεῖν ἐκεῖ (οἱ δὲ ἀδελφοὶ οὐκ ἔγνωσαν τίς ἐστιν ὁ πρεσβύτερος). καὶ καθήμενοι ἐν τῷ πλοίῳ, ἐλάλουν λόγους πατέρων τῆς ἐκκλησίας, καὶ ἐκ τῆς γραφῆς, καὶ πάλιν περὶ τοῦ ἔργου ἑαυτῶν. ὁ δὲ πρεσβύτερος ἐσιώπα[4]. ἐλθόντων δὲ αὐτῶν ἐπὶ τὴν γῆν, εὑρέθη καὶ ὁ πρεσβύτερος ὑπάγων πρὸς τὸν ἀββᾶν Ἀντώνιον. ὡς δὲ ἦλθον πρὸς αὐτόν, λέγει αὐτοῖς ὁ Ἀντώνιος· "καλὸν ἀδελφὸν εὕρετε, τὸν πρεσβύτερον τοῦτον." εἶπε δὲ καὶ τῷ πρεσβυτέρῳ· "καλοὺς ἀδελφοὺς εὗρες μετὰ σοῦ, ἀββᾶ." λέγει ὁ πρεσβύτερος· "καλοὶ μέν εἰσιν, ἀλλ᾽ ἡ οἰκία αὐτῶν οὐκ ἔχει θύραν[5], καὶ πᾶς ὁ θέλων εἰσέρχεται καὶ λύει[6] τὸν ὄνον[7]." τοῦτο δὲ ἔλεγεν ὅτι πάντα τὰ ἐρχόμενα εἰς τὸ στόμα αὐτῶν λαλοῦσιν.

---

4 σιωπάω 'I remain silent'

5 θύρα, -ας, ἡ 'door'

6 λύω 'I loose'

7 ὄνος, -ου, ὁ 'donkey'

6. Wild Men of the Desert

Macarius the Egyptian (c. 300–391) was the founder of Scetis. He had been a camel-driver and niter smuggler before taking monastic orders, and he knew the desert like few others. Here he is depicted in characteristic humility.

Ἦλθέ ποτε Μακάριος ὁ Αἰγύπτιος ἀπὸ Σκήτεως εἰς τὸ ὄρος τῆς Νιτρίας ἵνα προσκυνήσῃ τὸν Θεὸν μετὰ τοῦ ἀββᾶ Παμβώ· καὶ λέγουσιν αὐτῷ οἱ πρεσβύτεροι· "εἰπὲ ῥῆμα τοῖς ἀδελφοῖς, ὦ ἄνθρωπε τοῦ Θεοῦ." ὁ δὲ εἶπεν· "ἐγὼ <u>οὔπω</u>[1] γέγονα ἄνθρωπος Θεοῦ, ἀλλ᾽ εἶδον ἀνθρώπους Θεοῦ. καθήμενος γάρ ποτε ἐν τῇ οἰκίᾳ μου ἐν Σκήτει, ἤκουσα τῆς φωνῆς τῆς ψυχῆς μου λεγούσης· ἄπελθε εἰς τὴν <u>ἔρημον</u>[2], καὶ ἴδε τί βλέπεις ἐκεῖ.᾽ ἔμεινα δὲ <u>διακρινόμενος</u>[3] ἐν τούτῳ <u>ἔτη</u>[4] πολλά λέγων· 'μὴ ἀπὸ δαιμονίων ἐστίν;' καὶ ὡς οὐκ <u>ἐπαύετο</u>[5] ἡ ψυχή μου ταῦτα λέγουσα, ἀλλὰ καὶ μᾶλλον παρεκάλει, ἀπῆλθον εἰς τὴν <u>ἔρημον</u>· καὶ εὗρον ἐκεῖ θάλασσαν ὑδάτων, καὶ <u>νῆσον</u>[6] ἐν μέσῳ αὐτῆς· καὶ ἦλθον τὰ <u>θηρία</u>[7] τῆς <u>ἐρήμου</u> πιεῖν ἐξ αὐτῆς. καὶ εἶδον ἐν μέσῳ αὐτῶν δύο ἀνθρώπους <u>γυμνοὺς</u>[8]

---

1 οὔπω 'not yet'

2 ἔρημος, -ου, ἡ 'desert'

3 διακρίνομαι 'I judge; hesitate'

4 ἔτος, -ους, τό 'year'

5 παύομαι 'I stop; cease'

6 νῆσος, -ου, ἡ 'island'

7 θηρίον, -ου, τό 'beast; animal'

8 γυμνός, -ή, -όν 'naked'

καὶ ἐφοβήθην· ἐδόκουν γὰρ ὅτι πνεύματά εἰσιν.
αὐτοὶ δέ ὡς εἶδόν με φοβούμενον, ἐλάλησαν πρὸς
μέ· ʽμὴ φοβοῦ· καὶ ἡμεῖς ἄνθρωποί ἐσμεν.ʼ καὶ εἶπον
αὐτοῖς· ʽ<u>πόθεν</u>[9] ἐστὲ καὶ πῶς ἤλθετε εἰς τὴν <u>ἔρημον</u>
ταύτην;ʼ καὶ εἶπον· ʽἐζήσαμέν ποτε μετ᾽ ἀδελφῶν
πολλῶν· καὶ <u>συνεθέμεθα</u>[10], καὶ ἐξήλθομεν ὧδε· ἰδοὺ
<u>τεσσαράκοντα</u>[11] ἔτη. καὶ ὁ μὲν εἷς Αἰγύπτιος, ὁ δὲ
ἕτερος Λιβυκὸς ὑπάρχει.ʼ καὶ ἐπερώτησάν με καὶ
αὐτοί, λέγοντες· ʽπῶς ὁ κόσμος; καὶ εἰ ἔρχεται τὸ
ὕδωρ κατὰ καιρὸν αὐτοῦ, καὶ εἰ ἔχει ὁ κόσμος τὴν
εἰρήνην αὐτοῦ;ʼ καὶ εἶπον αὐτοῖς· ʽ<u>ναί</u>[12].ʼ κἀγὼ αὐτοὺς
ἠρώτησα· ʽπῶς δύναμαι ἄνθρωπος Θεοῦ γενέσθαι;ʼ
καὶ λέγουσί μοι· ʽἐὰν μὴ ἀφήσῃ τις πάντα τὰ τοῦ
κόσμου, οὐ δύναται γενέσθαι ἄνθρωπος Θεοῦ.ʼ καὶ
εἶπον αὐτοῖς· ʽἐγὼ δὲ παιδίον εἰμί, καὶ οὐ δύναμαι ὡς
ὑμεῖς.ʼ καὶ εἶπόν μοι καὶ αὐτοί· ʽκαὶ ἐὰν οὐ δύνασαι ὡς
ἡμεῖς, κάθου ἐν τῇ οἰκίᾳ σου, καὶ προσεύχου περὶ τῶν
ἁμαρτιῶν σου.ʼ καὶ ἠρώτησα αὐτούς· ʽὅταν γίνηται
<u>χειμών</u>[13], οὐ κακῶς ἔχετε; καὶ ὅταν γίνηται <u>θέρος</u>[14],
οὐκ ἀπόλλυται ἡ σάρξ ὑμῶν;ʼ οἱ δὲ εἶπον· ʽὁ Θεὸς
ἐποίησεν ἡμῖν τὴν χάριν ταύτην, ἵνα καὶ τῷ <u>χειμῶνι</u>
τὸ <u>ψῦχος</u>[15] καὶ τῷ <u>θέρει</u> τὸ <u>καῦμα</u>[16] φέρει τὰ σώματα
ἡμῶν.ʼ διὰ τοῦτο εἶπον ὑμῖν, ἀδελφοί, ὅτι <u>οὔπω</u>
γέγονα ἄνθρωπος Θεοῦ, ἀλλ᾽ εἶδον τοιούτους.ʼʼ

---

9 πόθεν ʻfrom whereʼ

10 συντίθημι ʻI make an agreementʼ

11 τεσσαράκοντα ʻfortyʼ

12 ναί ʻyesʼ

13 χειμών, -ῶνος, ὁ ʻbad weather; winterʼ

14 θέρος, -ους, τό ʻharvest; summerʼ

15 ψῦχος, -ους, τό ʻcoldʼ

16 καῦμα, -τος, τό ʻheatʼ

7. Three Visions

Many of the monks were visited by ecstatic visions, which were prized for their spiritual instruction. As in this story, however, the monks would often tell of their experiences in the third person, in order to avoid conceit (cf. 2 Cor 12:2: I knew a man in Christ [...] caught up to the third heaven.)

Ἔλεγεν ὁ ἀββᾶς Δανιὴλ ὅτι· "εἶπεν ἡμῖν ὁ ἀββᾶς Ἀρσένιος τὸν λόγον τοῦτον ὡς περὶ ἄλλου τινός (ἀλλὰ αὐτὸς ἦν ὁ ἀββᾶς Ἀρσένιος ὁ ποιήσας)· ὅτι καθημένου τινὸς πρεσβυτέρου ἐν τῇ οἰκίᾳ αὐτοῦ, ἦλθεν αὐτῷ φωνὴ λέγουσα· 'ἐλθὲ, καὶ <u>δείξω</u>[1] σοι τὰ ἔργα τῶν ἀνθρώπων.' καὶ ἀναστὰς ἐξῆλθε· καὶ ἤγαγεν αὐτὸν τὸ πνεῦμα εἰς τόπον τινά, καὶ <u>ἔδειξεν</u> ἄνδρα <u>κόπτοντα</u>[2] <u>ξύλα</u>[3]. καὶ συνῆγεν αὐτὰ ὁ ἀνὴρ ἐπὶ τὸ αὐτὸ καὶ ἐποίει <u>φορτίον</u>[4] μέγα· ἤθελε δὲ αὐτὸ <u>βαστάσαι</u>[5], καὶ οὐκ ἠδύνατο· οὐδὲ ἦρε <u>ξύλα</u> ἐκ τοῦ <u>φορτίου</u>, ὥστε δύνασθαι αὐτὸν <u>βαστάσαι</u>· ἀλλὰ πάλιν <u>ἔκοπτε</u> καὶ ἄλλα <u>ξύλα</u>, καὶ ἔβαλλεν ἐπὶ τὸ <u>φορτίον</u>. τοῦτο δὲ ἐπὶ πολὺ ἐποίει, καὶ τὸ <u>φορτίον</u> μεῖζον ἐγένετο. καὶ πορευθέντος ὀλίγον πάλιν <u>ἔδειξεν</u> αὐτῷ ἄνθρωπον ἱστάμενον ἐπὶ <u>φρέατος</u>[6] ὕδατος.

---

1 δείκνυμι 'to show'

2 κόπτω 'I cut'

3 ξύλον, -ου, τό 'wood'

4 φορτίον, -ου, τό 'burden'

5 βαστάζω 'I lift and carry'

6 φρέαρ, -τος, τό 'well'

καὶ ἔφερεν ὕδωρ ἐξ αὐτῆς, καὶ ἔβαλλεν εἰς <u>σκεῦος</u>[7]
<u>σχισμένον</u>[8]. καὶ τὸ αὐτὸ ὕδωρ εἰσελθὸν εἰς τὸ <u>σκεῦος</u>
πάλιν εἰς τὸ <u>φρέαρ</u> ἐξῆλθεν. καὶ λέγει αὐτῷ πάλιν ἡ
φωνή· 'ἐλθέ, <u>δείξω</u> σοι ἄλλο.' καὶ θεωρεῖ ἱερὸν καὶ
δύο ἄνδρας καθημένους ἐφ' <u>ἵππων</u>[9] ἐνώπιον αὐτοῦ.
καὶ <u>ἐβάσταζον</u> οἱ δύο <u>ξύλον</u> μέγα, ὡς <u>ζυγὸν</u>[10] ἐν
μέσῳ αὐτῶν· ἤθελον δὲ εἰς τὸ ἱερὸν εἰσελθεῖν, καὶ
οὐκ ἠδύναντο, ὅτι τὸ <u>ξύλον</u> ἐν μέσῳ αὐτῶν ἦν. καὶ
οὐκ ἤθελεν ὁ εἷς ἑαυτὸν <u>ταπεινῶσαι</u>[11] καί, καταβὰς
ἀπὸ τοῦ ἵππου, ἀκολουθῆσαι τῷ ἑτέρῳ καὶ ἐνέγκαι
τὸ <u>ξύλον</u> ἐπ' εὐθείας· καὶ διὰ τοῦτο ἔμειναν ἔξω
τοῦ ἱεροῦ. 'οὗτοί εἰσι,' φησίν, 'οἱ <u>βαστάζοντες</u> ὡς
δικαιοσύνης <u>ζυγὸν</u>, <u>μέγα φρονοῦντες</u>[12] ἐν τῇ ἑαυτῶν
δόξῃ. καὶ οὐκ <u>ἐταπεινώθησαν</u> ἵνα <u>μετανοήσωσιν</u>[13] καὶ
πορευθῶσι τῇ ὁδῷ τοῦ Χριστοῦ· διὸ καὶ μένουσιν
ἔξω τῆς βασιλείας τοῦ Θεοῦ. ὁ δὲ <u>κόπτων</u> τὰ <u>ξύλα</u>
ἄνθρωπός ἐστιν ἐν ἁμαρτίαις πολλαῖς· καὶ οὐ
<u>μετανοεῖ</u>, ἀλλὰ καὶ ἄλλα κακὰ βάλλει ἐπὶ τὰς πρώτας
αὐτοῦ ἁμαρτίας. καὶ ὁ τὸ ὕδωρ φέρων ἄνθρωπός
ἐστι, καλὰ μὲν ἔργα ποιῶν, ἀλλὰ εἶχεν ἐν αὐτοῖς καὶ
πονηρὰ ἔργα· καὶ διὰ τοῦτο ἀπώλεσε σὺν αὐτοῖς
καὶ τὰ καλὰ αὐτοῦ ἔργα. δεῖ οὖν πάντα ἄνθρωπον
βλέπειν πρὸς τὰ ἔργα αὐτοῦ, ἵνα μὴ ἀπόληται.'"

---

7 σκεῦος, -ου, τό 'jar; vessel'

8 σχίζομαι 'I crack; divide'

9 ἵππος, -ου, ὁ 'horse'

10 ζυγός, -οῦ, ὁ 'yoke'

11 ταπεινόω 'I humble'

12 μέγα φρονέω 'I am proud'

13 μετανοέω 'I repent'

8. Sunday Worship

Ἔλεγον πάλιν περὶ τοῦ ἀββᾶ Ἀρσενίου ὅτι· τὰ σάββατα τὴν νύκτα ἔστηκεν ἕως πάλιν ἦλθεν τὸ φῶς τῆς ἡμέρας. καὶ ἀφῆσας τὸ φῶς <u>ὀπίσω</u> αὐτοῦ, <u>ἐξέτεινε</u> τὰς χεῖρας αὐτοῦ εἰς τὸν οὐρανὸν προσευχόμενος, ἕως πάλιν ἔπεσεν τὸ φῶς ἐπὶ τὸ πρόσωπον αὐτοῦ· καὶ οὕτως τὴν ἡμέραν πᾶσαν προσευξάμενος, τότε ἐκαθέζετο.

9. The Power of Sight

Ἔλεγον περί τινος πατρὸς μεγάλου· ὅτι ἦν καθήμενος ἐν τῷ Πορφυρίτῃ, καὶ ὅταν ἦρεν τοὺς ὀφθαλμοὺς εἰς τὸν οὐρανὸν πάντα ἐθεώρει τὰ ἐν τῷ οὐρανῷ, καὶ εἰ ἐθεώρει εἰς τὴν γῆν, ἔβλεπε τὰς <u>ἀβύσσους</u>[1] καὶ πάντα τὰ ἐν αὐταῖς.

---

1   ἄβυσσος, -ου, ἡ 'the abyss'

10. The Destruction of Scetis

Scetis, the desert city of the monks, was sacked several times. This story probably refers to the first devastation by nomads around AD 407/8.

Ἔλεγον περὶ μεγάλου πρεσβυτέρου ἐν τῇ Σκήτει ὅτι, ὅταν ἐξήρχετό τις ἐκ τοῦ κόσμου θέλων παρὰ τοῖς ἀδελφοῖς μένειν, ἐποίουν αὐτῷ οἱ ἄλλοι ἀδελφοὶ οἰκίαν. καὶ ἐξήρχετο οὗτος ὁ πρεσβύτερος μετὰ χαρᾶς καὶ αὐτὸς πρῶτος θεὶς τὸν θεμέλιον² οὐκ ἀπήρχετο, ἕως οὗ ἐτελειώθη³ τὸ ἔργον. ποτὲ οὖν ἐξελθὼν ποιῆσαι οἰκίαν, οὐκ ἐχάρη ἀλλὰ ἐλυπεῖτο⁴ πολύ. καὶ λέγουσιν αὐτῷ οἱ ἀδελφοί· "τί λυπούμενος εἶ, ἀββᾶ;" ὁ δὲ εἶπεν· "μέλλει ὁ τόπος οὗτος ἀπολέσθαι, τέκνα. ἐγὼ γὰρ εἶδον ὅτι πῦρ μέγα ἐγένετο ἐν Σκήτει. καὶ λαβόντες οἱ ἀδελφοὶ ὕδωρ καὶ ἱμάτια πάντα ἐποίουν ἵνα σβέσωσιν⁵ αὐτό. καὶ πάλιν ἠγέρθη πῦρ, καὶ πάλιν ἔσβεσαν αὐτό. τὸ δὲ τρίτον ἐγένετο, καὶ ἐπλήρωσε πᾶσαν τὴν Σκῆτιν, καὶ οὐκ ἠδυνήθη σωθῆναι οὐδέν. διὰ τοῦτο λυποῦμαι."

---

2 θεμέλιος, -ου, ὁ 'foundation'

3 τελειόω 'I complete'

4 λυπέομαι 'I be sad'

5 σβέννυμι 'I quench'

11. The Insistent Beggar

The monks made their living by weaving baskets or plaiting rope and selling their wares at the market. Here Abba Agatho has a fortuitous encounter on such an expedition.

Εἰσῆλθέ ποτε ὁ ἀββᾶς Ἀγάθων εἰς τὴν πόλιν πωλῆσαι[1] τὰς σπυρίδας[2] αὐτοῦ, καὶ εὑρίσκει τινὰ χωλὸν[3] παρὰ τὴν ὁδόν. λέγει αὐτῷ ὁ χωλός· "ποῦ ὑπάγεις;" λέγει αὐτῷ ὁ ἀββᾶς Ἀγάθων· "εἰς τὴν πόλιν πωλῆσαι σπυρίδας." λέγει αὐτῷ· "κύριε, ἄρόν με ἐκεῖ." καὶ ἤνεγκεν[4] αὐτὸν εἰς τὴν πόλιν. λέγει αὐτῷ· "ὅπου πωλεῖς τὰς σπυρίδας, ἐκεῖ με θές[5]." ἐποίησε δὲ οὕτως. καὶ ὅτε ἐπώλησε σπυρίδα, ἔλεγεν αὐτῷ ὁ χωλός· "πόσου[6] ἐπώλησας αὐτήν;" καὶ ἔλεγε· "τόσου[7]." καὶ ἔλεγεν αὐτῷ· "ἀγόρασόν[8] μοι ἄρτον." καὶ ἠγόρασε. καὶ πάλιν ἐπώλησεν ἄλλην σπυρίδα. καὶ ἔλεγε· "καὶ ταύτην πόσου;" καὶ ἔλεγε· "τόσου." καὶ ἔλεγεν αὐτῷ· "ἀγόρασόν μοι τοῦτο." καὶ ἠγόρασε. μετὰ οὖν τὸ πωλῆσαι πάσας τὰς σπυρίδας, ἤθελεν ὁ ἀββᾶς Ἀγάθων ἀπελθεῖν. καὶ λέγει αὐτῷ ὁ χωλός· "ὑπάγεις;" λέγει αὐτῷ· "ἦλθεν ἡ ὥρα." καὶ λέγει· "κύριε, εἰ

---

1 πωλέω 'I sell'

2 σπυρίς, -ίδος, ἡ 'basket'

3 χωλός, ή, όν 'lame'

4 ἤνεγκεν 'he carried' (3 per. sing. aor. indic. φέρω 'I carry')

5 θές 'put' (sing. aor. impv. τίθημι 'I put, place')

6 πόσου 'for how much' (neut. gen. sing. πόσος 'how much')

7 τόσου 'for this much' (neut. gen. sing. τόσος 'this much')

8 ἀγοράζω 'I buy'

δύνασαι, ἆρον πάλιν ὅπου με εὖρες." καὶ <u>ἤνεγκεν</u>
αὐτὸν εἰς τὸν τόπον αὐτοῦ. καὶ λέγει αὐτῷ· "χάριν
ἔχεις, Ἀγάθων, παρὰ Κυρίῳ ἐν οὐρανῷ καὶ ἐπὶ γῆς."
καὶ ἄρας τοὺς ὀφθαλμοὺς αὐτοῦ οὐδένα εἶδεν· ἦν γὰρ
ἄγγελος Κυρίου ὃς ἦλθεν ἰδεῖν τὴν ἀγάπην αὐτοῦ.

12. The Forgetful Father

*The Desert Fathers strove to be as meek and gentle
toward others as they were severe on themselves. Heart-
warming tales such as these punctuate the starkness of
their monastic rigor.*

Πρεσβύτερός τις ἦν ἐν Σκήτει τῆς Αἰγύπτου· τὸ
μὲν σῶμα αὐτοῦ μεγάλην εἶχεν δύναμιν, ἀλλὰ οὐ
τὸ πνεῦμα. οὐ γὰρ <u>ἐμνημόνευε</u>⁹ οὐδενός, ἀλλὰ τὰ
πάντα <u>ἐπελανθάνετο</u>¹⁰. ἀπῆλθεν οὖν ποτέ πρὸς τὸν
ἀββᾶν Ἰωάννην, ἐρωτῆσαι αὐτὸν περὶ τῆς <u>μνείας</u>¹¹·
καὶ ἀκούσας παρ' αὐτοῦ λόγον, <u>ἐπέστρεψεν</u>¹² εἰς τὸν
οἶκον αὐτοῦ, καὶ εὐθὺς <u>ἐπελάθετο</u> ὃ εἶπεν αὐτῷ ὁ
ἀββᾶς Ἰωάννης. καὶ ἀπῆλθε πάλιν ἐρωτῆσαι αὐτόν·
ἀκούσας δὲ παρ' αὐτοῦ τὸν αὐτὸν λόγον, πάλιν
<u>ἐπέστρεψεν</u>. ὡς δὲ ἦλθεν εἰς τὸν ἴδιον οἶκον πάλιν
<u>ἐπελάθετο</u>. καὶ οὕτω δὲ ἐπὶ πολὺ ἀπερχόμενος,
<u>ἐπιστρέψας</u> οὐκ ἠδύνατο <u>μνημονεύειν</u> τοῦ λόγου.

---

9   μνημονεύω 'I remember'

10 ἐπιλανθάνομαι 'I forget'

11 μνεία, ας, ἡ 'memory'

12 ἐπιστρέφω 'I turn, return'

μετὰ δὲ ταῦτα προσελθὼν τῷ ἀββᾷ Ἰωάννῃ εἶπεν·
"οἶδας, ἀββᾶ, ὅτι <u>ἐπελαθόμην</u> πάλιν ὅ μοι εἶπας; ἀλλ᾽
ἵνα μὴ σοι <u>κόπους παρέχω</u>[1], οὐκ ἦλθον." λέγει αὐτῷ
ὁ ἀββᾶς Ἰωάννης· "ὕπαγε, <u>ἄψον</u>[2] <u>λύχνον</u>[3]." καὶ <u>ἦψεν</u>.
εἶπε καὶ αὐτῷ πάλιν· "φέρε ἄλλους <u>λύχνους</u>, καὶ <u>ἄψον</u>
ἐξ αὐτοῦ." ἐποίησε δὲ οὕτως. καὶ εἶπεν ἀββᾶς Ἰωάννης
τῷ πρεσβυτέρῳ· "μὴ τί ποτε <u>κόπους παρεῖχες</u> τῷ
<u>λύχνῳ</u>, ὅτι <u>ἦψας</u> ἐξ αὐτοῦ τοὺς ἄλλους <u>λύχνους</u>;"
λέγει· "οὐχί." εἶπε δὲ ὁ ἀββᾶς· "οὕτως οὐδὲ Ἰωάννης·
ἐὰν ἡ Σκῆτις ἔρχηται πρὸς μὲ πᾶσα, οὐ μή με ἐκβαλεῖ
ἐκ τῆς χάριτος τοῦ Χριστοῦ. διό, ὅταν θέλεις, ἔρχου,
μηδὲν φοβούμενος." καὶ οὕτω δι᾽ ἀγάπης τῶν δύο
ἀνδρῶν, ἔδωκεν ὁ Θεὸς τῷ πατρὶ δύναμιν τῆς <u>μνείας</u>.
τοῦτο δὲ ἦν ἔργον τῶν Σκητιωτῶν, διδόναι χάριν τοῖς
μὴ ἔχουσι καὶ διδάσκειν ἀλλήλους πρὸς τὸ ἀγαθόν.

---

1 κόπους παρέχω 'I make trouble for; I annoy'

2 ἄπτω 'I light'

3 λύχνος, ου, ὁ 'lamp'

13. The Ship at Sea

Ἐγένετο ἀδελφόν τινα εἰς ἁμαρτίαν πεσεῖν, ὅτε ἔμεινε παρὰ τῶν μαθητῶν τοῦ ἀββᾶ Ἠλίτ· οἱ δὲ ἄλλοι ἀδελφοὶ ἐξέβαλον αὐτὸν ἔξω εἰς τὴν <u>ἔρημον</u>[4]. πορευθεὶς οὖν ἀπῆλθεν εἰς ὄρος πρὸς τὸν ἀββᾶν Ἀντώνιον. καὶ μείναντος τοῦ ἀδελφοῦ χρόνον πολὺν πρὸς αὐτὸν, ἀπέστειλεν αὐτὸν ὁ ἀββᾶς Ἀντώνιος πάλιν πρὸς τοὺς ἀδελφοὺς αὐτοῦ. οἱ δὲ ἰδόντες αὐτὸν οὐκ ἠσπάσαντο, ἀλλὰ πάλιν ἐξέβαλον· ὁ δὲ ἦλθεν πρὸς τὸν ἀββᾶν Ἀντώνιον λέγων· "οὐκ ἠθέλησάν με δέξασθαι, πάτερ." ἀπέστειλεν οὖν ὁ πρεσβύτερος λέγων· "εἰπὲ αὐτοῖς ταύτην τὴν παραβολήν· 'πλοῖον <u>ἐβασανίζετο</u>[5] ἐν τῇ θαλάσσῃ, καὶ ἀπώλεσε τὰ ἐν αὐτῷ ἀγαθὰ, καὶ <u>μόλις</u>[6] ἐσώθη αὐτὸ ἐπὶ τὴν γῆν· ὑμεῖς δὲ τὰ σωθέντα ἐπὶ τὴν γῆν πάλιν θέλετε ἐκβαλεῖν εἰς τὴν θάλασσαν.'" οἱ δὲ ἀκούσαντες ὅτι ὁ ἀββᾶς Ἀντώνιος αὐτὸν ἀπέστειλεν, εὐθὺς ἐδέξαντο αὐτόν.

---

4 ἔρημος, -ου, ἡ 'desert'

5 βασανίζομαι 'to be tormented'

6 μόλις 'with difficulty; hardly'

14. Doers, Not Hearers

Ἔλεγεν ὁ ἀββᾶς Εὐλόγιος ὁ τοῦ Ἐνάτου ὅτι ἔμενεν ἀδελφός τις ἐν τοῖς Κελλίοις ὃς οὐδὲν ἐποίει νυκτὸς καὶ ἡμέρας εἰ μὴ <u>ἀνεγίνωσκεν</u>. καὶ ἀναστάς ποτε συνήγαγεν ὅσα εἶχεν <u>βιβλία</u> καὶ ἔδωκεν τοῖς λοιποῖς ἀδελφοῖς. καὶ λαβὼν τὸ ἱμάτιον αὐτοῦ ἀπῆλθεν εἰς τὴν <u>ἔρημον</u>. προσῆλθεν δὲ αὐτῷ ὁ ἀββᾶς Ἰσαὰκ καὶ λέγει αὐτῷ· "<u>ποῦ</u> πορεύῃ, τέκνον;" καὶ ἀπεκρίθη ὁ ἀδελφὸς λέγων· "ἰδοὺ οὐδὲν ποιῶ, πάτερ, νυκτὸς καὶ ἡμέρας εἰ μὴ ἀκούω μόνον τοὺς λόγους τῶν <u>βιβλίων</u>· νῦν δὲ θέλω λοιπὸν ἄρξασθαι καὶ τοῖς ἔργοις ποιεῖν ἃ ἤκουσα ἐκ τῶν <u>βιβλίων</u>." καὶ προσευξάμενος ὑπὲρ αὐτοῦ ἀπέλυσεν αὐτόν.

15. Forgive Us Our Debts

Ἦλθέ ποτε ἀδελφός τις πρὸς τὸν ἀββᾶν Σιλουανὸν
εἰς τὸ ὄρος εἰς Πανεφὼ καὶ λέγει αὐτῷ· "ἀββᾶ,
ἐχθρὸν¹ ἔχω πολλὰ κακὰ ποιήσαντά μοι· καὶ γὰρ καὶ
ἐξέβαλέ με ἐκ τοῦ οἴκου μου ὡς ἤμην ἐν τῷ κόσμῳ
καὶ τὸν πάντα χρόνον ἤθελέ με ἀπολέσαι. καὶ νῦν
θέλω παραδοῦναι αὐτὸν τῷ ἄρχοντι ἵνα ἐκδικήσῃ²
με." λέγει αὐτῷ ὁ πρεσβύτερος· "κατὰ τὸ θέλημά σου,
τέκνον, ποίησον." λέγει ὁ ἀδελφός· "ναί³, ἀββᾶ, καὶ
ἐὰν οὕτως πάθῃ, μᾶλλον σωθήσεται ἡ ψυχὴ αὐτοῦ."
λέγει ὁ πρεσβύτερος· "καθὼς δοκεῖ σοι, τέκνον,
ποίησον." καὶ λέγει ὁ ἀδελφὸς τῷ πρεσβυτέρῳ·
"ἀνάστα, πάτερ, προσευξώμεθα, καὶ τότε ἀπέρχομαι
πρὸς τὸν ἄρχοντα." καὶ ἀνέστη ὁ πρεσβύτερος, καὶ
λεγόντων αὐτῶν τὸ 'Πάτερ Ἡμῶν', ὡς ἤμελλον
λέγειν· *'καὶ ἄφες ἡμῖν τὰ ὀφειλήματα⁴ ἡμῶν ὡς
καὶ ἡμεῖς ἀφίεμεν τοῖς ὀφειλέταις⁵ ἡμῶν,'* εἶπεν ὁ
πρεσβύτερος· *'ὡς οὐδὲ ἡμεῖς ἀφίεμεν τοῖς ὀφειλέταις
ἡμῶν,'* καὶ λέγει ὁ ἀδελφὸς τῷ πρεσβυτέρῳ· "μὴ
οὕτως, πάτερ." καὶ εἶπεν ὁ πρεσβύτερος· "ἀλλὰ πῶς,
τέκνον; ἐὰν γὰρ πρὸς τὸν ἄρχοντα θέλεις ἀπελθεῖν,
ἵνα ἐκδικήσῃ σε, οὐ μὴ προσεύξηται ὑπέρ σου
Σιλουανός." καὶ μετανοήσας⁶ ὁ ἀδελφὸς ἀφῆκε τῷ
ἐχθρῷ αὐτοῦ.

---

1 ἐχθρός, -οῦ, ὁ 'enemy'

2 ἐκδικέω 'I grant justice, avenge'

3 ναί 'yes'

4 ὀφείλημα, -τος, τό 'debt'

5 ὀφειλέτης, -ου, ὁ 'debtor'

6 μετανοέω 'to repent'

16. The Tax Collector and the Corpse

Ἔλεγέ τις τῶν πατέρων ὅτι ἦν τις <u>τελώνης</u>[1] πεμφθεὶς παρὰ τοῦ βασιλέως. καὶ ἐν τῇ ὁδῷ εὗρέ τινα νεκρὸν ἐπὶ τῆς γῆς <u>κείμενον</u>[2] <u>γυμνόν</u>[3]. καὶ ἰδὼν αὐτὸν λέγει τῷ δούλῳ αὐτοῦ· "λάβε τὸν <u>ἵππον</u>[4] καὶ πορεύου ὀλίγον." ὁ δὲ <u>τελώνης</u> καταβὰς ἀπὸ τοῦ <u>ἵππου</u>, ἔλαβεν τὸ ἱμάτιον αὐτοῦ τὸ καλὸν καὶ βαλὼν ἐπὶ τὸ <u>γυμνὸν</u> σῶμα ἀπῆλθεν. πάλιν μεθ᾽ ἡμέρας, ἀπεστάλη ὁ αὐτὸς <u>τελώνης</u> εἰς γῆν ἑτέραν. ἐγένετο δὲ ἐξελθόντος αὐτοῦ ἐκ τῆς πόλεως, καὶ ἔπεσεν ἀπὸ τοῦ <u>ἵππου</u> καὶ <u>κατεάγη</u>[5] ὁ ποὺς αὐτοῦ. καὶ φέρει ὁ δοῦλος αὐτὸν εἰς τὸν οἶκον αὐτοῦ, καὶ παρεκάλεσε τοὺς <u>ἰατρούς</u>[6]. μετὰ δὲ ὀλίγας ἡμέρας, <u>μέλας</u>[7] ἐγένετο ὁ ποὺς αὐτοῦ. καὶ ἰδόντες οἱ <u>ἰατροὶ</u> <u>μέλανα</u> γενηθέντα τὸν πόδα αὐτοῦ, ἔλεγον πρὸς ἀλλήλους κατ᾽ ἰδίαν ὅτι <u>ἐκκοπῆναι</u>[8] δεῖ τὸν πόδα· εἰ δὲ μή, πονηρὸν μέλλει ποιεῖν ὅλον τὸ σῶμα καὶ ἀποθνήσκει ὁ ἄνθρωπος. καὶ λέγουσιν αὐτῷ· "ἐρχόμεθα <u>πρωῒ</u>[9] καὶ ἐροῦμέν σοι πῶς δοκεῖ ἡμῖν τὰ περὶ σου." ὁ δὲ <u>τελώνης</u> λέγει τῷ δούλῳ αὐτοῦ ἵνα ἐξέλθη <u>ὀπίσω</u>[10] τῶν <u>ἰατρῶν</u>

---

1 τελώνης, ου, ὁ 'tax collector'

2 κείμενος 'lying'

3 γυμνός, ή, όν 'naked'

4 ἵππος, ου, ὁ 'horse'

5 κατάγνυμι 'I break'

6 ἰατρός, οῦ, ὁ 'doctor'

7 μέλας, αινα, αν 'black'

8 ἐκκόπτω 'I cut off'

9 πρωῒ 'in the morning; early'

10 ὀπίσω 'behind'

καὶ ἀκούσῃ παρ᾽ αὐτῶν τὴν ἀλήθειαν. καὶ λέγουσιν αὐτῷ· "ὁ πούς τοῦ κυρίου σου <u>μέλας</u> ἐγένετο καὶ ἐὰν μὴ <u>ἐκκοπῇ</u>, ἀπόλλυται ὁ ἄνθρωπος· ἐρχόμεθα <u>πρωῒ</u> καὶ ὃ θέλει ὁ Θεὸς ποιοῦμεν." καὶ εἰσέρχεται ὁ δοῦλος <u>λυπούμενος</u>[11] πρὸς τὸν κύριον αὐτοῦ λέγων ὅτι· "οὕτως δοκοῦσι περὶ σοῦ." ὁ δὲ ἀκούσας <u>ἐταράχθη</u>[12], καὶ οὕτως <u>ἐλυπεῖτο</u> ὥστε οὐκ <u>ἐκοιμήθη</u>[13]. ἦν δὲ φῶς ὀλίγον ἐν τῷ οἴκῳ ἔτι <u>φαῖνον</u>[14]. περὶ δὲ τὰς μέσας νύκτας, ὁρᾷ ἄνθρωπον ἐρχόμενον πρὸς αὐτὸν καὶ λέγοντα αὐτῷ· "τί <u>λυπῆσαι</u>; τί <u>ἐταράχθης</u>;" ὁ δὲ λέγει· "κύριε, οὐ θέλεις ἵνα <u>λυπηθῶ</u> καὶ <u>ταραχθῶ</u>, ὅτι <u>κατεάγην</u>, καὶ τοιοῦτό τι λέγουσι περὶ ἐμοῦ οἱ <u>ἰατροί</u>;" καὶ λέγει αὐτῷ ὁ <u>φανείς</u>· "ἄφες ἴδω τὸν πόδα σου." καὶ <u>ἀλείφει</u>[15] αὐτὸν καὶ λέγει· "ἀνάστα νῦν καὶ περιπάτει." καὶ λέγει ὁ <u>τελώνης</u>· "<u>κατεάγη</u> καὶ οὐ δύναμαι." καὶ λέγει αὐτῷ· "<u>κράτησόν</u>[16] μου τῆς χειρός." καὶ <u>κρατήσας</u>, περιεπάτει ὀλίγον. καὶ λέγει αὐτῷ ὁ <u>φανείς</u>· "ἔτι οὐ δύνασαι καλῶς περιπατεῖν; κάθου πάλιν ἵνα ἴδω σου τὸν πόδα." καὶ πάλιν <u>ἀλείφει</u> αὐτοῦ καὶ τὸν ἕτερον πόδα. καὶ λέγει αὐτῷ· "ἔγειρε νῦν, περιπάτει." καὶ ἀναστὰς περιεπάτησεν καλῶς. καὶ λέγει αὐτῷ· "κάθου πάλιν." καὶ εἶπεν αὐτῷ τινὰς λόγους περὶ <u>ἐλέους</u>[17], ὅτι εἶπεν ὁ Κύριος· *μακάριοι οἱ*

---

11 λυπέομαι 'I am sad'

12 ταράσσομαι 'I am distressed'

13 κομάομαι 'I fall asleep'

14 φαίνω 'I shine' (mid. 'appear')

15 ἀλείφω 'I anoint (with oil)'

16 κρατέω 'I grab; hold'

17 ἔλεος, -ους, τό 'mercy'

ἐλεήμονες¹, ὅτι αὐτοὶ ἐλεηθήσονται², καὶ ἀνήλεος³
ἡ κρίσις⁴ τῷ μὴ ποιήσαντι ἔλεος, καὶ ὅσα τοιαῦτα.
καὶ λέγει αὐτῷ· "χαῖρε." λέγει ὁ τελώνης· "ὑπάγεις;"
ἀποκρίνεται αὐτῷ· "τί ἔτι θέλεις· νῦν γὰρ καλῶς
ἔχεις." λέγει αὐτῷ ὁ τελώνης· "εἰπέ μοι τίς εἶ· οἶδά
σε γὰρ ὅτι ὁ Θεός σε ἔπεμψεν." λέγει αὐτῷ· "βλέψον
εἰς ἐμέ. οὐκ ἐπιγινώσκεις⁵ τοῦτο τὸ ἱμάτιον;" λέγει
αὐτῷ· "ναί⁶, κύριε, ἐμόν ἐστιν." καὶ λέγει αὐτῷ
ἐκεῖνος· "ἐγώ εἰμι ὃν εἶδες νεκρὸν κείμενον ἐν τῇ
ὁδῷ, καὶ ἔβαλες ἐπ' ἐμὲ τὸ ἱμάτιον· καὶ ἀπέστειλέ με
ὁ Θεὸς πρός σε. ἔχε οὖν χάριν τῷ Θεῷ εἰς τὸν αἰῶνα."
καὶ ἐξῆλθε πάλιν καθὼς καὶ εἰσῆλθεν. ὁ δὲ τελώνης
ἐδόξαζεν τὸν Θεόν, παρ' οὗ καταβαίνει πᾶν ἀγαθόν.

---

1 ἐλεήμων, -ον 'merciful'

2 ἐλεάω 'I show mercy'

3 ἀνήλεος, -ον 'merciless'

4 κρίσις, -εως, ἡ 'judgment'

5 ἐπιγινώσκω 'I know; recognize'

6 ναί 'yes'

17. The Dead Man's Pledge

Ἔλεγεν ὁ ἀββᾶς Σισόης· "ὅτε ἤμην ἐν Σκήτει μετὰ
τοῦ Μακαρίου, ἐξήλθομεν <u>θερίσαι</u>⁷ μετʼ αὐτοῦ, ἑπτὰ
<u>ὀνόματα</u>⁸· καὶ ἰδοὺ <u>χήρα</u>⁹ συνάγουσα ἦν <u>ὀπίσω</u>¹⁰
ἡμῶν, καὶ οὐκ <u>ἐπαύετο</u>¹¹ <u>κλαίουσα</u>¹². ἐκάλεσεν οὖν
ὁ Μακάριος τὸν κύριον τοῦ <u>ἀγροῦ</u>¹³, καὶ εἶπεν αὐτῷ·
ʽτί ἔχει ἡ γυνὴ αὕτη, ὅτι οὐ <u>παύεται</u> <u>κλαίουσα;</u>ʼ λέγει
αὐτῷ· ʽὅτι ὁ ἀνὴρ αὐτῆς εἶχε <u>παραθήκην</u>¹⁴ τινός,
καὶ ἀπέθανεν εὐθύς, καὶ οὐκ εἶπεν ἀποθανὼν <u>ποῦ</u>¹⁵
ἔθηκεν αὐτήν· νῦν δὲ θέλει ὁ κύριος τῆς <u>παραθήκης</u>
λαβεῖν αὐτὴν καὶ τὰ τέκνα αὐτῆς εἰς δούλους.ʼ λέγει
αὐτῷ ὁ πρεσβύτερος· ʽεἰπὲ αὐτῇ ἵνα ἔλθῃ πρὸς ἡμᾶς,
ὅπου <u>ἀναπαυόμεθα</u>¹⁶ τὸ <u>καῦμα</u>¹⁷.ʼ καὶ ἐλθούσης
τῆς γυναικός, εἶπεν αὐτῇ ὁ πρεσβύτερος· ʽγύναι, τί
οὐ <u>παύει</u> οὕτως <u>κλαίουσα;</u>ʼ καὶ εἶπεν· ʽὁ ἀνήρ μου
ἀπέθανε λαβὼν <u>παραθήκην</u> τινός, καὶ οὐκ εἶπεν
ἀποθνήσκων <u>ποῦ</u> <u>ἔκρυψεν</u>¹⁸ αὐτήν.ʼ καὶ εἶπεν ὁ
πατὴρ πρὸς αὐτήν· ʽἐλθέ, ἄγε ἡμᾶς ὅπου ἔθηκας τὸν

---

7 θερίζω ʻI harvestʼ

8 ὄνομα, -τος, τό ʻnameʼ (can also mean ʻpersonʼ, as in Acts 1:15)

9 χήρα, -ας, ἡ ʻwidowʼ

10 ὀπίσω ʻbehindʼ

11 παύομαι ʻI stop; ceaseʼ

12 κλαίω ʻI cryʼ

13 ἀγρός, -οῦ, ὁ ʻfieldʼ

14 παραθήκη, -ης, ἡ ʻpledge; depositʼ

15 ποῦ ʻwhereʼ

16 ἀναπαύομαι ʻI restʼ

17 καῦμα, -τος, τό ʻheat; noondayʼ

18 κρύπτω ʻI hideʼ

ἄνδρα σου.' καὶ λαβὼν τοὺς ἀδελφοὺς μεθ' ἑαυτοῦ,
ἐξῆλθε σὺν αὐτῇ. καὶ ἐλθόντων ἐπὶ τὸν τόπον, εἶπεν
αὐτῇ ὁ πρεσβύτερος· 'ὕπαγε εἰς τὴν οἰκίαν σου.' καὶ
προσευξαμένων αὐτῶν, ἐκάλεσεν ὁ πρεσβύτερος τὸν
νεκρὸν λέγων· 'ἀδελφέ, <u>ποῦ</u> ἔθηκας τὴν <u>παραθήκην</u>
τοῦ κυρίου σου;' ὁ δὲ ἀποκριθεὶς εἶπεν· 'ἐν τῷ
οἴκῳ μου <u>κέκρυπται</u>, ὑπὸ τὸν πόδα τῆς <u>κλίνης</u>[1].'
καὶ λέγει αὐτῷ ὁ πατήρ· '<u>ἀναπαύου</u> πάλιν ἕως τῆς
ἐσχάτης ἡμέρας.' ἰδόντες δὲ οἱ ἀδελφοὶ φοβηθέντες
ἔπεσον πρὸς τοὺς πόδας αὐτοῦ. καὶ εἶπεν αὐτοῖς
ὁ πρεσβύτερος· 'οὐ δι' ἐμὲ γέγονε τοῦτο· οὐδὲν
γάρ εἰμι. ἀλλὰ διὰ τὴν <u>χήραν</u> καὶ τὰ τέκνα ὁ Θεὸς
ἐποίησεν. τοῦτο δέ ἐστι τὸ μέγα· θέλει ὁ Θεὸς ἵνα μὴ
ἔχῃ ἡ ψυχή ἁμαρτίαν. καὶ εἴ τι ἂν αἰτήσηται λαμβάνει.
ἐλθόντες δὲ, λέγετε τῇ <u>χήρᾳ</u> <u>ποῦ</u> ἐστίν ἡ <u>παραθήκη</u>.'
ἡ δὲ λαβοῦσα αὐτὴν, ἔδωκε τῷ κυρίῳ αὐτῆς, καὶ οὐκ
ἔλαβεν αὐτοὺς εἰς δούλους. καὶ πάντες οἱ ἀκούσαντες
ἐδόξασαν τὸν Θεόν."

---

1 κλίνη, -ης, ἡ 'bed'

18. The Lapsed Bishop

Not all Christians withstood the Diocletian Persecution of 303–313. Some, like the bishop in this story, renounced their faith and sacrificed to Caesar. The fate of these apostates was a major point of dispute in the Donatist Controversy of the fourth century.

Ἔλεγε πάλιν ἄλλος πρεσβύτερος, ὃς <u>ἐπίσκοπος</u>[2] ἦν ἐν πόλει Ὀξυρύγχῳ, τὸν λόγον τοῦτον (ὡς ἑτέρου τινὸς ἔλεγεν, ἦν δὲ αὐτὸς ὁ τοῦτο πεποιηκώς). "ἔδοξέ μοι," φησί, "ποτε εἰς τὴν <u>ἔρημον</u>[3] εἰσελθεῖν, ἰδεῖν εἰ εὕρω τινὰ πιστὸν δοῦλον τοῦ Θεοῦ. λαβὼν οὖν ὀλίγους ἄρτους καὶ ὡς ἡμερῶν τριῶν ὕδωρ, ἐπορεύθην. μετὰ δὲ τὰς τρεῖς ἡμέρας <u>ὑστέρησεν</u>[4] τὸ ὕδωρ· καὶ <u>οὐκέτι</u>[5] οἶδα τί ποιήσω. καὶ πιστεύσας εἰς τὸν Κύριον, παρέδωκα ἐμαυτὸν εἰς τὴν χεῖρα αὐτοῦ καὶ ἐπορεύθην ἄλλας τρεῖς ἡμέρας, μὴ πίνων ὕδωρ. τὸ δὲ σῶμά μου λοιπὸν τὸν <u>κόπον</u>[6] τῆς ὁδοῦ <u>οὐκέτι</u> ἔφερεν, καὶ πεσὼν ἐπὶ τῆς γῆς <u>ἐκοιμήθην</u>[7]. ἐλθὼν δὲ ἀνήρ τις, ἔθηκε τὴν χεῖρα αὐτοῦ ἐπὶ τὸ στόμα μου. εὐθὺς δὲ εὗρον δύναμιν ὥστε δοκεῖν ὅτι <u>οὔπω</u>[8] ἐπορεύθην οὐδέν. ὡς οὖν εἶδον τὴν δύναμιν ταύτην

---

2 ἐπίσκοπος, ου, ὁ 'overseer; (later) bishop'

3 ἔρημος, -ου, ἡ 'desert'

4 ὑστερέω 'I run out'

5 οὐκέτι 'no longer'

6 κόπος, ου, ὁ 'work, labor'

7 κοιμάομαι 'I fall asleep'

8 οὔπω 'not yet'

πληρῶσάν με, ἀναστὰς <u>διηρχόμην</u>[1] τὴν <u>ἔρημον</u>.
μετὰ δὲ ἄλλας τέσσαρες ἡμέρας πάλιν ὕδατος
<u>ὑστερήσας</u>, <u>ἐξέτεινα</u>[2] εἰς τὸν οὐρανὸν τὰς χεῖράς
μου. καὶ ἰδοὺ ὁ ἀνὴρ ὁ τὸ πρότερον δούς μοι δύναμιν
καὶ πάλιν ἔθηκε τὴν χεῖρα αὐτοῦ ἐπὶ τὸ στόμα μου.
μετὰ δὲ ἡμέρας <u>δεκαεπτά</u>[3], εὑρίσκω οἶκον καὶ
<u>δένδρον</u>[4] καὶ ὕδωρ καὶ ἄνδρα στήκοντα· αἱ <u>τρίχες</u>[5]
τῆς κεφαλῆς αὐτοῦ ἦσαν ἱμάτια αὐτῷ (ἦν γὰρ
<u>γυμνός</u>[6])· <u>λευκαὶ</u>[7] πᾶσαι ὑπῆρχον. ὡς δὲ εἶδέ με,
ἔστη προσευχόμενος· καὶ <u>τελέσας</u>[8] τὸ 'ἀμήν', ἔγνω
εἶναί με ἄνθρωπον καὶ οὐ δαιμόνιον. <u>κρατήσας</u>[9]
οὖν τῆς χειρός μου, ἠρώτα λέγων· "πῶς ὧδε ἦλθες,
καὶ εἰ ἔτι καλῶς ἔχει πάντα τὰ ἐν τῷ κόσμῳ, καὶ εἰ
ἔτι εἰσίν οἱ <u>διωγμοί</u>[10];" ἐγὼ δὲ εἶπον· "δι' ὑμᾶς τῶν
μετὰ ἀληθείας προσκυνούντων τὸν Θεόν, ταύτην
τὴν <u>ἔρημον</u> <u>διέρχομαι</u>· τὸ δὲ τοῦ <u>διωγμοῦ</u> οὐκέτι
ἐστίν, διὰ τῆς χάριτος τοῦ Χριστοῦ. εἰπὲ δέ μοι καὶ
αὐτὸς πῶς ὧδε ἦλθες." ὁ δὲ ἤρξατο <u>κλαίειν</u>[11] λέγων·
"ἐγὼ <u>ἐπίσκοπος</u> ἤμην, καὶ <u>διωγμοῦ</u> γενομένου εἰς
μεγάλην ἁμαρτίαν ἔπεσα καὶ ἡ πίστις μου ἀπώλετο·

---

1 διέρχομαι 'I go through'

2 ἐκτείνω 'I stretch out'

3 δεκαεπτά 'fifteen'

4 δένδρον 'tree'

5 θρίξ, τριχός, ἡ 'hair'

6 γυμνός, ή, όν 'naked'

7 λευκός, -ή, -όν 'white'

8 τελέω 'I finish'

9 κρατέω 'I grab; hold'

10 διωγμός, οῦ, ὁ 'persecution'

11 κλαίω 'to cry, mourn'

μὴ δυνηθεὶς γὰρ <u>ὑπενεγκεῖν</u>[12] τὸν <u>βασανισμὸν</u>[13],
<u>ἠρνησάμην</u>[14] τὸν Χριστὸν καὶ <u>ἔθυσα</u>[15] τῷ Καίσαρι.
ὡς δὲ ἐν ἐμαυτῷ ἐγενόμην <u>ἐπέγνων</u>[16] τὴν ἁμαρτίαν
μου καὶ ἔδωκα ἐμαυτὸν ἀποθανεῖν ἐν τῇ <u>ἐρήμῳ</u>
ταύτῃ. καί εἰμι ὧδε μένων <u>ἔτη</u>[17] <u>τεσσαράκοντα</u>
<u>ἐννέα</u>[18], καὶ <u>κλαίων</u> καὶ παρακαλῶν τὸν Θεὸν ἵνα
ἀφεθῶσί μοι αἱ ἁμαρτίαι· καὶ τὴν μὲν ζωὴν ἐδίδου
μοι ὁ Κύριος ἐκ τῶν καρπῶν τοῦ <u>δένδρου</u> τούτου.
πίστιν δὲ οὐκ ἔλαβον ὅτι ἀφίενταί μοι αἱ ἁμαρτίαι,
ἕως <u>ἐτῶν</u> <u>τεσσαράκοντα ὀκτώ</u>[19]· πρὸ μόνον ὀλίγων
ἡμερῶν παρεκλήθην." ὡς δὲ ταῦτα ἔλεγεν, εὐθὺς
ἀναστὰς ἀπῆλθεν ἵνα προσεύχηται ἐπὶ πολλὰς
ὥρας. ὡς δὲ <u>ἐτέλεσε</u> τὸ 'ἀμήν', ἦλθε πάλιν πρός με.
θεωρήσας δὲ τὸ πρόσωπον αὐτοῦ ἐφοβήθην· ἦν γὰρ
γενόμενος ὡς πῦρ. εἶπεν δέ μοι· "μὴ φοβοῦ. καὶ γὰρ
ὁ Κύριος ἀπέσταλκέ σε ἵνα <u>θάψῃς</u>[20] μου τὸ σῶμα."
ὡς δὲ <u>ἐτέλεσε</u> λαλῶν, εὐθὺς <u>ἐκτείνας</u> τὰς χεῖρας
καὶ τοὺς πόδας, ἀφῆκεν τὸ πνεῦμα. θεὶς δὲ ἐγὼ τὸ
ἱμάτιόν μου, <u>μέρος</u>[21] ἓν ἐμαυτῷ μὲν τηρήσας, τὸ δὲ
ἕτερον <u>μέρος</u> ἔβαλον ἐπὶ τὸ σῶμα αὐτοῦ τὸ ἅγιον,
καὶ ἔθηκα αὐτὸ ἐν τῇ γῇ. ὡς δὲ <u>ἔθαψα</u> αὐτόν, εὐθὺς
ὁ οἶκος ἔπεσεν καὶ τὸ <u>δένδρον</u> οὐκέτι εὑρέθη. ἐγὼ

---

12 ὑποφέρω 'I endure'

13 βασανισμός, οῦ, ὁ 'torture'

14 ἀρνέομαι 'I deny'

15 θύω 'I sacrifice'

16 ἐπιγινώσκω 'I know; recognize'

17 ἔτος, -ους, τό 'year'

18 τεσσαράκοντα ἐννέα 'forty nine'

19 τεσσαράκοντα ὀκτώ 'forty eight'

20 θάπτω 'I bury'

21 μέρος, -ους, τό 'part; piece'

δὲ πολλὰ <u>ἔκλαυσα</u>, παρακαλῶν τὸν Θεὸν ἵνα δῷ μοι
τοὺς καρποὺς τοῦ <u>δένδρου</u> καὶ μείνω ἐν τῷ τόπῳ
ἐκείνῳ ὅσον χρόνον ἔτι ζῶ. ὡς δὲ οὐκ ἐγένετο τοῦτο,
εἶπον ἐν ἑαυτῷ μὴ εἶναι θέλημα Θεοῦ. προσευξάμενος
οὖν ἦλθον πάλιν ἐπὶ τὴν <u>οἰκουμένην</u>[1]. καὶ ἰδοὺ ὁ
ἄνθρωπος ὁ τὸ πρῶτον θεὶς τὴν χεῖρα ἐπὶ τὸ στόμα
μου ἦλθέ μοι πάλιν καὶ ἔδωκέν μοι δύναμιν. καὶ οὕτως
ἀπελθὼν πρὸς τοὺς ἀδελφοὺς εἶπον αὐτοῖς περὶ
τοῦ πρεσβυτέρου ἐκείνου, καὶ παρεκάλουν αὐτοὺς
πιστεύειν καὶ ἐν τῇ ἀληθείᾳ μένοντες εὑρίσκειν τὸν
Θεόν.

19. Cyril of Alexandria and the Heretic

Cyril of Alexandria (c. 376–444) was a central figure
in the Nestorian debates of the fifth century and the
Council of Ephesus in 431. Here he is depicted with
Solomonian wisdom as leading a wayward monk from
Lower Egypt to the truth about the person of Melchize-
dek.

Ὁ ἀββᾶς Δανιὴλ <u>διηγήσατο</u>[2] περὶ ἄλλου τινὸς
πρεσβυτέρου μεγάλου, καθημένου ἐν τῇ κάτω
Αἰγύπτῳ, ὃς ἔλεγεν ὅτι ὁ Μελχισεδὲκ υἱός ἐστι τοῦ
Θεοῦ. οὗτος ὁ πατὴρ ἐν τούτῳ μὲν <u>ἐπλανήθη</u>[3],
ἀλλὰ ὡς πρὸς τὰ ἄλλα ἀνὴρ πιστὸς καὶ δίκαιος ἦν.

---

1 οἰκουμένη, ης, ἡ 'the inhabited world'

2 διηγέομαι 'I tell (a story)'

3 πλανέομαι 'I wander; err; am deceived'

καὶ ἤκουσεν ὁ μακάριος Κύριλλος ὁ ἐπίσκοπος[4]
ὁ ἐν Ἀλεξανδρείᾳ περὶ αὐτοῦ καὶ ἔπεμψεν πρὸς
αὐτὸν ἵνα ἔλθῃ. οἶδε δὲ ὅτι ἄνθρωπος Θεοῦ ἐστίν ὁ
πρεσβύτερος, καὶ εἴ τι αἰτεῖ τῷ Θεῷ, ἀποκαλύπτει[5]
αὐτῷ· καὶ ὅτι ἐν τούτῳ μόνῳ ἐπλανήθη ὁ πατὴρ,
τὰ δὲ ἀλλὰ καλῶς ἔχων, ἐχρήσατο[6] ὁ Κύριλλος
τοιαύτῃ σοφίᾳ λέγων· "ἀββᾶ, παρακαλῶ σε,
ὅτι δύο διαλογισμοὺς[7] ἔχω· ὁ μέν λέγει, ὅτι· 'ὁ
Μελχισεδὲκ υἱὸς τοῦ Θεοῦ ἐστι,' ὁ δὲ λέγει, ὅτι· 'οὐ,
ἀλλ' ἄνθρωπός ἐστιν ἀρχιερεὺς τοῦ Θεοῦ.' ἐγὼ δὲ
μὴ εἰδὼς τίς ἐστιν ἡ ἀλήθεια ἀπέστειλα πρὸς σὲ, ἵνα
αἰτήσῃς τῷ Θεῷ, ἵνα σοι ἀποκαλύψῃ περὶ τούτου."
ὁ δὲ πρεσβύτερος ἐπίστευεν ὅτι ὁ Θεὸς αὐτῷ
ἀποκριθήσεται καὶ εἶπεν μετὰ παρρησίας[8]· "δός μοι
τρεῖς ἡμέρας, κἀγὼ ἐρωτῶ τὸ Θεὸν περὶ τούτου, καὶ
ἐρῶ σοι τίς ἐστιν." ἀπελθὼν οὖν ἠρώτα τὸν Θεὸν περὶ
τοῦ ῥήματος τούτου. καὶ ἐλθὼν μετὰ τρεῖς ἡμέρας,
λέγει τῷ μακαρίῳ Κυρίλλῳ ὅτι· "ἄνθρωπός ἐστιν ὁ
Μελχισεδέκ." καὶ εἶπεν αὐτῷ ὁ ἐπίσκοπος· "πῶς οἶδας,
ἀββᾶ;" ὁ δὲ εἶπεν· "ὁ Θεὸς ἀπεκάλυψέ μοι πάντας
τοὺς πατριάρχας[9], οὕτως ἕνα ἕκαστον ἀναβαίνοντα
ἐνώπιόν μου, ἀπὸ Ἀδὰμ ἕως Μελχισεδέκ· καὶ γίνωσκε
ὅτι οὕτως ἐστίν." ἀπελθὼν οὖν καὶ αὐτὸς ἐκήρυσσεν
ὅτι ἄνθρωπός ἐστιν ὁ Μελχισεδέκ. καὶ ἐχάρη
μεγάλως ὁ μακάριος Κύριλλος.

---

4 ἐπίσκοπος, ου, ὁ 'overseer; (later) bishop'

5 ἀποκαλύπτω 'I reveal'

6 χράομαι 'I use'

7 διαλογισμός, -οῦ, ὁ 'thought'

8 παρρησία 'boldness; confidence'

9 πατριάρχης, ου, ὁ 'patriarch'

20. Honest Abba John

The monks lived at a subsistence level, selling their wares in exchange for their daily bread. This stark reliance on God for provision characterized the monastic way of life.

Ἔλεγέ τις τῶν πατέρων περὶ τοῦ ἀββᾶ Ἰωάννου τοῦ Πέρσου, ὅτι ἀνὴρ δίκαιος ἦν καὶ πιστότατος· οὗτος δὲ ἔμενεν ἐν Ἀραβίᾳ τῆς Αἰγύπτου. ἐδανείσατο¹ δέ ποτε παρὰ ἀδελφοῦ ἀργύριον² ἕν, καὶ ἠγόρασε³ λίνον⁴, ἵνα ποιήσῃ τὸ ἔργον αὐτοῦ. καὶ ἦλθεν ἀδελφὸς παρακαλῶν αὐτὸν καὶ λέγων· 'δός μοι, ἀββᾶ, ὀλίγον λίνον, ἵνα ποιήσω ἐμαυτῷ ἱμάτιον." καὶ ἔδωκεν αὐτῷ μετὰ χαρᾶς. οὕτως δὲ καὶ ἄλλος ἦλθε παρακαλῶν αὐτόν· "δός μοι ὀλίγον λίνον, ἵνα ποιήσω ἐμαυτῷ ἱμάτιον." ἔδωκε δὲ καὶ αὐτῷ. καὶ ἄλλων αἰτησάντων, ἐδίδου πᾶσιν μετὰ χαρᾶς. τότε ἔρχεται ὁ κύριος τοῦ ἀργυρίου θέλων αὐτό. λέγει αὐτῷ ὁ πρεσβύτερος· "ἐγὼ ὑπάγω καὶ φέρω σοι αὐτό." καὶ μὴ ἔχων πόθεν⁵ ἀποδοῦναι⁶, ἀνέστη ἀπελθεῖν πρὸς τὸν ἀββᾶν Ἰάκωβον· ἤθελεν γὰρ παρακαλέσαι αὐτὸν δοῦναι αὐτῷ ἀργύριον ἕτερον, ἵνα ἀποδώσῃ τῷ ἀδελφῷ. καὶ πορευόμενος εὗρεν ἀργύριον ἐπὶ τῆς γῆς, καὶ οὐκ ἦρεν αὐτό. προσευξάμενος δέ,

---

1 δανίζω 'I lend' (mid. 'I borrow')
2 ἀργύριον, ου, τό 'silver (coin)'
3 ἀγοράζω 'I buy'
4 λίνον, ου, τό 'flax'
5 πόθεν 'from where'
6 ἀποδίδωμι 'I give back'

ἐπέστρεψεν⁷ εἰς τὸν ἑαυτοῦ οἶκον. καὶ ἦλθεν ὁ
ἀδελφὸς πάλιν κόπους αὐτῷ παρέχων⁸ περὶ τοῦ
ἀργυρίου λέγων ὅτι· "ἀπόδος ὃ ὀφείλεις⁹." καὶ
λέγει αὐτῷ ὁ πρεσβύτερος· "δός μοι χρόνον ὀλίγον
καὶ πάντα σοι ἀποδώσω." καὶ ἀπελθὼν πάλιν, εἶδε
τὸ ἀργύριον ἐπὶ τῆς γῆς ὅπου καὶ πρότερον ἦν· καὶ
πάλιν προσευξάμενος, ὑπέστρεψεν εἰς τὰ ἴδια. καὶ
ἰδοὺ πάλιν ἦλθεν ὁ ἀδελφὸς ὁ κόπους αὐτῷ παρέχων.
καὶ λέγει ὁ πρεσβύτερος ὅτι· "νῦν τοῦτο φέρω." καὶ
ἀναστὰς πάλιν, ἦλθε κατ' ἐκείνου τοῦ τόπου· καὶ
εὗρεν τὸ ἀργύριον ἐκεῖ ἐν τῇ ὁδῷ. καὶ προσευξάμενος
ἔλαβεν αὐτό. καὶ ἦλθε πρὸς τὸν ἀββᾶν Ἰάκωβον,
καὶ λέγει αὐτῷ· "ἀββᾶ, ἐρχόμενος πρὸς σὲ εὗρον
τὸ ἀργύριον τοῦτο ἐν τῇ ὁδῷ· κύριε, κήρυξον πρὸς
τοὺς λοιποὺς ἀδελφούς, μή τις ἀπώλεσεν αὐτό· καὶ
ἐὰν εὑρεθῇ ὁ κύριος αὐτοῦ, δὸς αὐτῷ." ἀπελθὼν
οὖν ὁ πρεσβύτερος, ἐπὶ τρεῖς ἡμέρας ἐκήρυξε· καὶ
οὐδεὶς εὑρέθη ὁ ἀπολέσας τὸ ἀργύριον. τότε λέγει
ὁ πρεσβύτερος τῷ ἀββᾷ Ἰακώβῳ· "εἰ οὖν οὐδεὶς
αὐτὸ ἀπώλεσε, δὸς αὐτὸ τούτῳ τῷ ἀδελφῷ· ὀφείλω
γὰρ αὐτῷ, καὶ ἐρχόμενος δανίσασθαι παρὰ σοῦ
ἀργύριον καὶ ἀποδοῦναι ὃ ὀφείλω, εὗρον αὐτό." καὶ
ἐθαύμασεν¹⁰ ὁ πατήρ, πῶς ὀφείλων καὶ εὑρὼν οὐκ
εὐθὺς ἔλαβε καὶ ἔδωκεν αὐτό. τοιαύτην γὰρ εἶχεν
ὁ ἀββᾶς Ἰωάννης ὁ Πέρσης καρδίαν ἀληθείας, ὅτι
εἰ ἤρχετό τις δανίσασθαί τι παρ' αὐτοῦ, οὐκ αὐτὸς
παρεῖχεν¹¹, ἀλλ' ἔλεγε τῷ ἀδελφῷ· "ὕπαγε, σεαυτῷ

---

7   ἐπιστρέφω 'I turn, return'

8   κόπους παρέχω 'I make trouble for; I annoy'

9   ὀφείλω 'I owe'

10 θαυμάζω 'I be amazed'

11 παρέχω 'I give to; offer'

ἆρον εἴ τινος <u>χρείαν</u>[1] ἔχεις." καὶ εἴ τις <u>ἀπεδίδου</u>,
ἔλεγεν αὐτῷ· "βάλε αὐτὸ πάλιν εἰς τὸν τόπον αὐτοῦ."
εἰ δὲ οὐδὲ <u>ἀπεδίδου</u> ὁ λαμβάνων, οὐδὲν ἔλεγεν αὐτῷ.

21. The Greedy Worldling

Ἦν ποτε ἀδελφός τις <u>νέος</u>[2] ὃς πρεσβύτερον εἶχεν
ἠγαπημένον. καὶ μετὰ χρόνον πολὺν προσῆλθεν αὐτῷ
ὁ ἀδελφὸς καί φησι πρὸς αὐτὸν ὁ πρεσβύτερος· "τί
ἐποίεις, τέκνον, τὸν <u>τοσοῦτον</u>[3] χρόνον;" ὁ δὲ λέγει·
"ἐν τῇ πόλει ἤμην, πάτερ, διά τινα <u>χρείαν</u>[4]." εἶπεν
οὖν αὐτῷ ὁ πρεσβύτερος· "καὶ τί ἀγαθὸν ἤκουσας ἢ
εἶδες ἐκεῖ;" λέγει ὁ ἀδελφός· "ἀγαθὸν μὲν οὐ πολύ, εἰ
μὴ <u>ὑπόκρισιν</u>[5] μόνην· ἓν δὲ <u>ἐθαύμασα</u>[6]. εἶδον γὰρ
ἀνθρώπους ἐν τῇ πόλει ζῶντας, ὅτι τῶν <u>ἀργυρίων</u>[7]
μᾶλλον <u>κατεφρόνουν</u>[8] ἢ ἡμεῖς οἱ ὧδε μένοντες
κατ᾽ ἰδίαν." λέγει ὁ πρεσβύτερος· "πῶς; εἰπέ μοι τὸν
λόγον." ἀπεκρίθη ὁ ἀδελφός· "δύο τινὰς <u>πλουσίους</u>[9]

---

1 χρεῖα, -ας, ἡ 'need'

2 νέος, -α, -ον 'new; young'

3 τοσοῦτος, -αύτη, -οῦτο 'so much'

4 χρεία, -ας, ἡ 'need; necessity'

5 ὑπόκρισις, -εως, ἡ 'hypocrisy'

6 θαυμάζω 'I wonder; admire'

7 ἀργύριον 'silver coin; (pl.) money'

8 καταφρονέω 'I scorn; do not care about'

9 πλούσιος, -ον 'rich, wealthy'

ἑώρακα¹⁰, καὶ ὁ εἷς ἔλεγεν ὅτι· 'σὺ ὀφείλεις¹¹ μοι
τοσαῦτα ἀργύρια· καὶ ἰδοὺ ἔχω βιβλίον¹² ἐν ᾧ ἐστί
γεγραμμένον, ὅτι ὤφειλεν ὁ πατήρ σου τοσαῦτα
δι᾽ ἐπαγγελίας.᾽ ὁ δὲ ἕτερος ἔλεγεν ὅτι· 'οὐχί, ἀλλὰ
ἤδη ἀπέδωκεν¹³ ὁ πατὴρ ὁ ἐμὸς τὸ ὀφείλημα¹⁴,
μηδὲν μὲν γράψας, ἀλλὰ εἰς τὴν δικαιοσύνην σου
πιστεύσας· πεπλήρωται οὖν ἡ ἐπαγγελία.᾽ καὶ ὡς
οὐκ ἔπειθον ἀλλήλους, ἔδοξεν αὐτοῖς ὀμόσαι¹⁵.
εἶπεν οὖν ὁ λεγόμενος¹⁶ ὀφείλων· 'ἐὰν ὀμόσω ὅτι
ἤδη ἀπεδόθη τὸ ὀφείλημα παρὰ τοῦ πατρός μου,
αὐτὸς δὲ τὰ ἀργύρια μὴ δῷ, δόξω τοῖς ἀνθρώποις
πλεονέκτης¹⁷ εἶναι. ἀλλὰ μᾶλλον οὕτως γενέσθω
ἡμῖν· ἢ ὀμνύω ἐγὼ ὅτι ἀπεδόθη σοι τὸ ὀφείλημα καὶ
δίδωμί σοι αὐτὰ πάλιν ἐκ δευτέρου, ἢ ὄμοσον σὺ ὅτι
ἔτι ὀφείλω σοι αὐτά, καὶ μηδὲν πλεῖον λάβῃς παρ᾽
ἐμοῦ, ἀλλὰ μὴ ζήτει τὰ ἀργύρια.᾽ καὶ ἐθαύμασαν
πάντες οἱ ἀκούσαντες τὴν μεγάλην σοφίαν τοῦ
ἀνδρός." λέγει οὖν ὁ πρεσβύτερος· "καὶ ὅτι νέος
εἶ, τέκνον, ἔδει σὲ θαυμάσαι. ἐγὼ δέ σε διδάξω, καὶ
εὑρήσεις μηδὲν ὂν μέγα, ἀλλὰ μόνης ὑποκρίσεως τὸ
πᾶν." λέγει ὁ ἀδελφός· "πῶς, πάτερ, εἰ κατεφρόνησε
τῶν τοσούτων ἀργυρίων, ἵνα μόνον μὴ δόξῃ τοῖς
ἀνθρώποις πλεονέκτης εἶναι;" λέγει ὁ πρεσβύτερος·
"ὁ καταφρονῶν ἀργυρίων ὀφείλει καὶ πᾶν ποιεῖν ἵνα

---

10 ἑώρακα 'I saw' (1 per. sing. perf. act. ind. ὁράω 'I see')

11 ὀφείλω 'I owe; ought to'

12 βιβλίον, -ου, τό 'scroll; record'

13 ἀποδίδωμι 'I give back; repay'

14 ὀφείλημα, -τος, τό 'debt'

15 ὀμνύω 'I swear (an oath)'

16 λεγόμενος 'so-called; alleged' (pres. masc. sing. part. λέγω 'I say')

17 πλεονέκτης, -ου, ὁ 'greedy man'

σωθῇ ἡ ψυχὴ τοῦ ἀδελφοῦ αὐτοῦ· τοῦ γὰρ Κυρίου καὶ
Θεοῦ ἡμῶν ἡ ἐντολὴ τὰ δύο ταῦτα λέγει· πρῶτον ἵνα
μὴ ἀγαπᾷ τις τὰ <u>ἀργύρια</u>, καὶ δεύτερον ἵνα ἀγαπήσῃ
αὐτοῦ τὸν ἀδελφόν. εἰ οὖν <u>ᾔδει</u>[1] ὁ ἄνθρωπος ἐκεῖνος
ὅτι ἤδη <u>ἀπέκδωκεν</u> ὁ πατὴρ αὐτοῦ τὸ <u>ὀφείλημα</u>, διὰ
τί εἶπεν ἵνα καὶ <u>ὀμόσῃ</u> καὶ πάλιν ἐκ δευτέρου αὐτὸ
<u>ἀποδώσῃ</u>; τί ἕτερον ἐποίει ἢ ὅτι <u>ἔδειξεν</u>[2] τὸν μὲν
ἀδελφὸν αὐτοῦ ὅτι πονηρός ἐστι καὶ <u>πλεονέκτης</u>
παρὰ Θεοῦ καὶ τῶν ἀνθρώπων; ἑαυτὸν δὲ <u>ἔδειξεν</u>
ὅτι <u>πλουσιώτατός</u> ἐστιν καὶ οὐδὲ <u>χρείαν</u> ἔχει τῶν
<u>ἀργυρίων</u>. τοῦτο δὲ πίστις καὶ σοφία οὐκ ἔστι, ἀλλὰ
<u>ὑπόκρισις</u>. ἡ γὰρ καρδία αὐτοῦ θέλει τὰ <u>ἀργύρια</u> καὶ
τὴν δόξαν παρὰ τῶν ἀνθρώπων, καὶ ὁ ὀφθαλμὸς
αὐτοῦ <u>πονηρός</u>[3] ἐστιν." λέγει ὁ ἀδελφός· "τί οὖν ἔδει
αὐτὸν ποιῆσαι; ὁ γὰρ ἄλλος ἄνθρωπος παρεκάλεσεν
αὐτὸν ἵνα <u>ὀμόσῃ</u>." ἀπεκρίθη ὁ πρεσβύτερος· "εἰ ἦν
δίκαιος, οὔτ' αὐτὸς <u>ὤμοσεν</u> ἂν οὔτε τὸν ἕτερον
παρεκάλεσεν ἵνα <u>ὀμόσῃ</u>, μάλιστα καὶ <u>πλούσιος</u> ὢν
καὶ εἰδὼς ὅτι ἤδη <u>ἀπέδωκε</u> τὸ <u>ὀφείλημα</u>." λέγει ὁ
ἀδελφός· "οὐκ οὖν ἔδει αὐτὸν ἐκ δευτέρου <u>ἀποδοῦναι</u>
τὰ <u>ἀργύρια</u>;" λέγει ὁ πατήρ· "καὶ οὐ <u>συμφέρει</u>[4] αὐτῷ
<u>ζημιωθῆναι</u>[5] καὶ μὴ <u>ὀμόσαι</u>, ἀλλὰ <u>κερδῆσαι</u>[6] καὶ
ἀγάπην; καὶ οὐ πάλιν λήμψεται πάντα ταῦτα ἐκ χειρὸς
τοῦ Θεοῦ ἐν τῇ βασιλείᾳ τοῦ οὐρανοῦ; διὸ οὐκ ἔδει
αὐτὸν δι' <u>ὑπόκρισιν</u> <u>δεῖξαι</u> τοῖς λοιποῖς ἀνθρώποις ὅτι
πονηρός ἐστιν ὁ τὰ <u>ἀργύρια</u> παρ' αὐτοῦ αἰτῶν· οὗτος

---

1 ᾔδει 'he knew' (3 per. sing. plpf. ind. οἶδα 'I know')

2 δείκνυμι 'I show'

3 ὁ πονηρὸς ὀφθαλμός 'envy; (lit.) evil eye'

4 συμφέρει 'it is better'

5 ζημιόομαι 'I suffer loss'

6 κερδαίνω 'I gain'

γὰρ ὁ ἀνὴρ οὐκ ἀγαπᾷ τὸν ἀδελφὸν αὐτοῦ. ὥστε
οὖν βλέπεις, τέκνον, ὡς ἐκεῖνα τὰ ἔργα θέλει ὁ Θεὸς
μόνα· τὰ καλῷ θελήματι γινόμενα καὶ ἐν πνεύματι
ἀγάπης τοῦ Θεοῦ ποιούμενα." καὶ ἀπῆλθεν ὁ ἀδελφὸς
χαίρων.

22. *Two Elders Quarrel*

Δύο πρεσβύτεροι ἦσαν χρόνον πολὺν μετ᾽ ἀλλήλων
καθήμενοι, καὶ <u>οὐδέποτε</u>[7] <u>μάχην</u>[8] ἐποίησαν. εἶπεν
δὲ ὁ εἷς τῷ ἑτέρῳ· "ποιήσωμεν καὶ ἡμεῖς <u>μάχην</u> ὡς οἱ
λοιποὶ ἄνθρωποι." ὁ δὲ ἀποκριθεὶς εἶπεν· "οὐκ οἶδα
πῶς γίνεται μάχη." ὁ δὲ εἶπεν αὐτῷ· "ἰδοὺ <u>τιθῶ</u>[9]
λίθον εἰς τὸ μέσον, κἀγὼ λέγω ὅτι 'ἐμόν ἐστιν,' καὶ σὺ
λέγεις ὅτι 'οὐχί, ἀλλὰ ἐμόν,' καὶ οὕτως γίνεται ἡ ἀρχή."
ἔθηκαν οὖν λίθον εἰς τὸ μέσον, καὶ λέγει ὁ εἷς· "τοῦτο
ἐμόν ἐστιν." εἶπεν δὲ ὁ ἄλλος· "οὐχί, ἀλλ᾽ ἐμόν." καὶ
εἶπεν ὁ ἕτερος· "εἰ σόν ἐστιν, ἆρον καὶ ὕπαγε." καὶ
ἀπῆλθον μηδὲν μετ᾽ ἀλλήλων εὑρόντες δι᾽ ὃ <u>μάχην</u>
ποιήσωσιν.

---

7 οὐδέποτε 'never'

8 μάχη, -ης, ἡ 'fight; quarrel'

9 τιθῶ 'let me put' (1 per. sing. pres. subj. τίθημι 'I put, place')

23. The Devil's Bags

Some of the most electric stories involve visions of demons. They constantly afflicted the monks, reminding them of their past lives in the world and the pleasures of sin, and deceiving or even physically assaulting them.

Ὁ ἀββᾶς Μακάριος εἶχέ ποτε ἐν τῇ ἐρήμῳ[1] τὸν οἶκον· καὶ ἦν μόνος ἐκεῖ μένων, οὐ μακρὰν[2] δὲ ἔμενον πλείονες ἀδελφοὶ ἐν ἄλλῃ ἐρήμῳ ἐπὶ τὸ αὐτό. ἐθεώρει δὲ ὁ πρεσβύτερος τὴν ὁδόν· καὶ ὁρᾷ τὸν Σατανᾶν πορευόμενον δι' αὐτῆς ἐν σώματι ἀνθρώπου. ἐφόρει[3] δὲ ἱμάτιον μέγα καὶ πήρας[4] εἶχε πολλὰς ἐν τοῖς χερσίν. καὶ λέγει αὐτῷ ὁ πρεσβύτερος ὁ μέγας· "ποῦ[5] πορεύῃ;" καὶ εἶπεν αὐτῷ· "ἀπέρχομαι ὑπομνῆσαι[6] τοὺς ἀδελφούς." ὁ δὲ πρεσβύτερος εἶπε· "καὶ ἵνα τί σοι αἱ πῆραι αὗται;" καὶ εἶπε· "ταύτας φέρω ἵνα δώσω τοῖς ἀδελφοῖς φαγεῖν." ὁ δὲ πρεσβύτερος εἶπε· "καὶ ταύτας πάσας;" ἀπεκρίθη· "οὕτως ἔχει· ἐὰν μὴ ἡ μία ἀρέσῃ[7] τινί, φέρω ἄλλην· ἐὰν δὲ μὴ καὶ αὕτη, δίδωμι ἄλλην· πάντως[8] δὲ ἐξ αὐτῶν κἂν[9] μία ἀρέσει αὐτῷ." καὶ ταῦτα εἰπὼν ἀπῆλθεν. ὁ δὲ πρεσβύτερος ἔμεινε

---

1 ἔρημος, -ου, ἡ 'desert'

2 μακράν 'far away'

3 φορέω 'I wear'

4 πήρα, -ας, ἡ 'sack; traveler's bag'

5 ποῦ 'where'

6 ὑπομιμνήσκω 'I remind'

7 ἀρέσκει + dat. 'I like'

8 πάντως 'certainly'

9 κἂν (καί + ἄν) 'even if; at least'

θεωρῶν τὴν ὁδόν, ἕως πάλιν ἐκεῖνος <u>ἐπέστρεψεν</u>[10].
καὶ ὡς εἶδεν αὐτὸν ὁ πρεσβύτερος, λέγει αὐτῷ·
"χαῖρε." ὁ δὲ ἀπεκρίθη· "<u>ποῦ</u> ἔστι μοι τὸ χαίρειν;"
λέγει αὐτῷ ὁ πρεσβύτερος· "διὰ τί;" ὁ δὲ λέγει· "ὅτι
πάντες <u>ἐχθροί</u>[11] μοι ἐγένοντο, καὶ οὐδείς μου ἀκούει."
λέγει αὐτῷ ὁ πατήρ· "οὐδένα οὖν δοῦλον ἔχεις ἐκεῖ;"
ὁ δὲ ἀπεκρίθη· "μόνον ἕνα ἔχω ἐκεῖ δοῦλον, καὶ <u>κἂν</u>
αὐτός μοι πείθεται καὶ ποιεῖ μου τὸ θέλημα· καὶ ὅταν
ὁρᾷ με, <u>στρέφεται</u>[12] ὡς ὁ <u>ἄνεμος</u>[13]." λέγει οὖν αὐτῷ ὁ
πατήρ· "καὶ τί ὄνομά ἐστιν τῷ ἀδελφῷ;" ὁ δὲ λέγει·
"Θεόπεμπτος." εἰπὼν δὲ ταῦτα ἀπῆλθεν. καὶ ἀναστὰς
ὁ ἀββᾶς Μακάριος καταβαίνει πρὸς τοὺς ἀδελφούς.
καὶ ἀκούσαντες οἱ ἀδελφοί, λαβόντες <u>βαῖα</u>[14] ἐξῆλθον
αὐτῷ εἰς <u>ἀπάντησιν</u>[15]. καὶ ἕκαστος ἤνοιξε τὸν
οἶκον αὐτοῦ, δοκῶν ὅτι παρ' αὐτῷ ἔμελλε μένειν
ὁ πρεσβύτερος. ὁ δὲ ἐζήτει τίς ἐστιν ὁ καλούμενος
Θεόπεμπτος. καὶ εὑρών, ἔμεινε παρ' αὐτῷ· ὁ δὲ
Θεόπεμπτος ἐδέξατο αὐτὸν χαίρων. κατ' ἰδίαν δὲ ὁ
πρεσβύτερος λέγει αὐτῷ· "πῶς τὰ κατὰ σέ, ἀδελφέ;"
ὁ δὲ εἶπεν· "σοῦ μὲν ὑπέρ μου προσεχομένου, καλῶς."
εἶπε δὲ ὁ πρεσβύτερος· "μὴ <u>πειράζει</u>[16] σε τὰ δαιμόνια;"
ὁ δὲ εἶπε· "τῇ χάριτι τοῦ Θεοῦ καλῶς ἔχω." ἐφοβεῖτο
γὰρ εἰπεῖν. λέγει αὐτῷ ὁ πατήρ· "ἰδοὺ χρόνον πολὺν
ἤδη μόνος ἐν τῇ <u>ἐρήμῳ</u> ζῶ, καὶ ἀγαπητός εἰμι παρὰ
πάντων, καὶ ἐμὲ τὸν πρεσβύτερον ἔτι <u>πειράζει</u>

---

10 ἐπιστρέφω 'I turn, return'

11 ἐχθρός, -οῦ, ὁ 'enemy; hostile'

12 στρέφομαι 'I turn around'

13 ἄνεμος, -ου, ὁ 'wind'

14 βαῖον, -ου, τό 'palm branch'

15 ἀπάντησις, -εως, ἡ 'meeting'

16 πειράζω 'I tempt; test'

τὸ πνεῦμα τῆς <u>πορνείας</u>[1]." ἀπεκρίθη λέγων καὶ ὁ
Θεόπεμπτος· "γίνωσκε, ἀββᾶ, καὶ ἐμὲ <u>πειράζει</u>." ὁ
δὲ πρεσβύτερος εἶπεν αὐτῷ καὶ ἕτερα πνεύματα, ἵνα
ποιήσῃ αὐτὸν εἰπεῖν τὴν ἀλήθειαν. τότε λέγει αὐτῷ·
"πῶς <u>νηστεύεις</u>[2];" ὁ δὲ λέγει αὐτῷ· "ἕως τῆς τρίτης
ὥρας." λέγει αὐτῷ ὁ πατήρ· "<u>νήστευε</u> μᾶλλον ἕως
νυκτός, καὶ προσεύχου· καὶ τήρει ἐν τῇ καρδίᾳ σου τὰ
ῥήματα τοῦ εὐαγγελίου καὶ τῶν ἄλλων γραφῶν· καὶ
ἐάν σοι προσέλθῃ πνεῦμα πονηρόν, μη βλέπε εἰς τὴν
γῆν, ἀλλὰ <u>πάντοτε</u>[3] πρὸς τὸν οὐρανόν· καὶ εὐθὺς ὁ
Κύριός μετά σου ἔσται." καὶ δοὺς ὁ πατὴρ τῷ ἀδελφῷ
τοὺς λόγους τούτους καὶ προσευξάμενος ὑπὲρ αὐτοῦ,
ἐξῆλθεν εἰς τὸν ἴδιον τόπον. καὶ θεωρῶν πάλιν τὴν
ὁδόν, ὁρᾷ ἐκεῖνον τὸ δαιμόνιον περιπατοῦν, καὶ λέγει
αὐτῷ· "<u>ποῦ</u> πάλιν ἀπέρχῃ;" ὁ δὲ λέγει· "<u>ὑπομνῆσαι</u>
τοὺς ἀδελφούς." καὶ ἀπῆλθεν. ὡς δὲ πάλιν <u>ἐπέστρεψε</u>,
λέγει αὐτῷ ὁ ἅγιος· "πῶς οἱ ἀδελφοί;" ὁ δὲ λέγει·
"κακῶς." ὁ δὲ πρεσβύτερος λέγει· "διὰ τί;" ὁ δὲ εἶπεν·
"<u>ἐχθροί</u> εἰσίν μοι πάντες καὶ τὸ μεῖζον κακὸν, ὅτι
καὶ ὃν εἶχον δοῦλον ἀκούοντά μου, καὶ αὐτὸς (οὐκ
οἶδα πῶς) ἀπώλετο. οὐδὲ αὐτός μοι πείθεται, ἀλλὰ
πάντων ἐχθρώτερος ἐγένετο· καὶ εἶπα <u>μηκέτι</u>[4] ἐκεῖ
πορεύεσθαι, εἰ μὴ μετὰ χρόνον πολύν." καὶ οὕτως
εἰπὼν ἀπῆλθεν, ἀφήσας τὸν πρεσβύτερον, καὶ ὁ ἅγιος
εἰσῆλθεν εἰς τὴν οἰκίαν αὐτοῦ.

---

1 πορνεῖα 'fornication'

2 νηστεύω 'I fast'

3 πάντοτε 'always'

4 μηκέτι 'not anymore'

24. The Council of Satan

Ἔλεγέ τις τῶν πρεσβυτέρων τῶν ἐν τῇ Θηβαΐδι
μενόντων ὅτι· "ἐγὼ ἤμην τέκνον προφήτου τῶν
Ἑλλήνων, ὃς τὰ δαιμόνια προσεκύνει. παιδίον οὖν
ὄν, ἐκαθήμην καθ' ἡμέραν καὶ εἶδον τὸν πατέρα
μου εἰσερχόμενον εἰς τὸ ἱερόν, ἵνα θυσίαν⁵ ποιήσῃ
τοῖς δαιμονίοις. καὶ ἐγὼ ἐν κρυπτῷ⁶ εἰσῆλθόν ποτε
ὀπίσω⁷ αὐτοῦ, ἵνα ἴδω τὸ γεγονός. καὶ εἶδον τὸν
Σατανᾶν καὶ πάντα τὸν ὄχλον τῶν δαιμονίων αὐτοῦ
ἐνώπιον τοῦ πατρός μου ἑστηκότας. καὶ ἰδοὺ ἄρχων
τις τοῦ Σατανᾶ ἐλθὼν προσεκύνει αὐτῷ. ἀποκριθεὶς
δὲ ὁ Διάβολος εἶπεν αὐτῷ· πόθεν⁸ σὺ ἔρχῃ;' ὁ δὲ
εἶπεν· ἐν ταύτῃ τῇ γῇ ἤμην, καὶ ἐποίησα πολέμους⁹,
καὶ αἵματα ἐξέχεα¹⁰ πολλὰ καὶ ἦλθόν σοι λόγον
δοῦναι.' καὶ εἶπεν αὐτῷ· πόσῳ¹¹ χρόνῳ τοῦτο
ἐποίησας;' ὁ δὲ εἶπεν· ἐν τριάκοντα¹² ἡμέραις.' ὁ δὲ
ἔδωκεν ἐντολὴν ἵνα μαστιγωθῇ¹³ ὁ ἄρχων καὶ εἶπεν·
τοσούτῳ¹⁴ χρόνῳ τοῦτο μόνον ἐποίησας;' καὶ ἰδοὺ
ἄλλο πνεῦμα πονηρὸν προσεκύνει αὐτῷ, καὶ λέγει
αὐτῷ ὁ Σατανᾶς· καὶ σὺ πόθεν ἔρχῃ;' ἀποκριθεὶς δὲ

---

5 θυσία, -ας, ἡ 'sacrifice'

6 ἐν κρυπτῷ 'in secret'

7 ὀπίσω 'behind'

8 πόθεν 'from where'

9 πόλεμος, -ου, ὁ 'war'

10 ἐκχέω 'I pour out'

11 πόσος 'how much'

12 τριάκοντα 'thirty'

13 μαστιγόω 'I whip'

14 τοσοῦτος 'this much'

τὸ δαιμόνιον εἶπεν· 'ἐν τῇ θαλάσσῃ ἤμην, καὶ ἐποίησα
<u>ἀνέμους</u> καὶ ἀπόλεσα πλοῖα, καὶ πολλοὺς ἀνθρώπους
ἀπέκτεινα, καὶ ἦλθόν σοι λόγον δοῦναι.' ὁ δὲ εἶπεν
αὐτῷ· '<u>πόσῳ</u> χρόνῳ τοῦτο ἐποίησας;' τὸ δὲ δαιμόνιον
εἶπεν· 'ἐν ἡμέραις <u>εἴκοσι</u>.' εἶπεν δὲ ἵνα <u>μαστιγωθῇ</u> καὶ
οὗτος λέγων· 'δια τί <u>τοσαύταις</u> ἡμέραις τοῦτο μόνον
ἐποίησας;' καὶ ἰδοὺ τὸ τρίτον ἐλθὸν προσεκύνει
αὐτῷ. εἶπεν δὲ καὶ τούτῳ· 'καὶ σὺ <u>πόθεν</u> ἔρχῃ;' καὶ
ἀποκριθεὶς τὸ δαιμόνιον εἶπεν· 'ἐν ταύτῃ τῇ πόλει
<u>γάμοι</u> ἐγένοντο, καὶ ἐποίησα <u>πόλεμον</u> καὶ αἵματα
<u>ἐξέχεα</u> πολλά, ἀποκτείνας τὸν <u>νυμφίον</u>¹ καὶ τὴν
<u>νύμφην</u>², καὶ ἦλθόν σοι λόγον δοῦναι.' ὁ δὲ εἶπεν·
'<u>πόσαις</u> ἡμέραις τοῦτο ἐποίησας;' καὶ εἶπεν· '<u>δέκα</u>.'
εἶπεν δὲ ἵνα <u>μαστιγωθῇ</u> καὶ οὗτος <u>τοσοῦτον</u> χρόνον
ἀπολέσαντα. ἔσχατος πάντων ἦλθεν καὶ ἕτερος
προσκυνῆσαι αὐτῷ. εἶπεν δέ· '<u>πόθεν</u> καὶ σὺ ἔρχῃ;' ὁ
δὲ εἶπεν· 'ἐν τῇ <u>ἐρήμῳ</u>³ ἤμην ἰδοὺ <u>τεσσαράκοντα</u>⁴
<u>ἔτη</u>⁵ μετ' ἀνθρώπου Θεοῦ ἑνός, καὶ τὴν νύκτα
ταύτην ἔπεσεν ὁ πρεσβύτερος εἰς ἁμαρτίαν μετὰ
γυναικός.' τοῦτο ἀκούσας, ἀναστάς, ἠσπάσατο αὐτόν,
καὶ ἄρας τὸν ἴδιον <u>στέφανον</u>, ἔθηκεν αὐτῷ ἐπὶ τὴν
κεφαλὴν, καὶ ἐκάθισεν αὐτὸν ἐν τῷ θρόνῳ αὐτοῦ
λέγων· 'ὅτι τὸ μέγα τοῦτο ἔργον ἠδυνήθης ποιῆσαι.'"
εἶπεν δὲ ὁ πρεσβύτερος· "τοῦτο ἐγὼ ἰδών, ἔλεγον·
'οὕτως μεγά ἐστι τὸ ἔθνος τῶν πατέρων τῆς <u>ἐρήμου</u>.'"
καὶ θέλοντος τοῦ Θεοῦ σῶσαί μου τὴν ψυχήν,
ἐξῆλθον εἰς τὴν <u>ἔρημον</u> ἵνα γένωμαι κἀγὼ ὡς ἐκεῖνοι.

---

1 νυμφίος, -ου, ὁ 'bridegroom'

2 νύμφη, -ης, ἡ 'bride'

3 ἔρημος, -ου, ἡ 'desert'

4 τεσσεράκοντα 'forty'

5 ἔτος, -ους, τό 'year'

25. Good Will

Εἶπέν τις τῶν πατέρων· "ἐὰν μὴ <u>μισήσῃς</u>[6] πρῶτον,
οὐ δύνασαι ἀγαπῆσαι· ἐὰν <u>μισήσῃς</u> τὴν ἁμαρτίαν,
ποιεῖς τὴν δικαιοσύνην, καθὼς γέγραπται· <u>*ἔκκλινον*</u>[7]
ἀπὸ κακοῦ καὶ ποίησον ἀγαθόν. ἀλλὰ καὶ ἐν πᾶσι
τούτοις, τὸ θέλημα ἐστὶν τὸ ζητουμένον παρὰ τῷ
Θεῷ. ὁ μὲν γὰρ Ἀδὰμ καὶ ἐν τῇ Ἐδὲμ ὤν, οὐκ ἐτήρησε
τὴν ἐντολὴν τοῦ Θεοῦ. ὁ δὲ Ἰὼβ εἰς χεῖρα τοῦ Σατανᾶ
παραδεδομένος καὶ ἐπὶ τῆς γῆς καθήμενος καὶ
κράζων, ἐτήρησε τὴν ἑαυτοῦ δικαιοσύνην. θέλημα
οὖν μόνον ἀγαθὸν ζητεῖ ὁ Θεὸς ἀπὸ τοῦ ἀνθρώπου,
καὶ ἵνα φοβῆται αὐτὸν ἐν παντὶ καιρῷ."

26. Short Sayings

Εἶπεν πρεσβύτερος· "ἐὰν κάθῃ ὧδε κατ᾽ ἰδίαν, μὴ
λέγεις ἐν τῇ καρδίᾳ σου ὅτι· "οὕτως μέγα ἔργον
ποιῶ." ἀλλὰ μᾶλλον ἔχε σεαυτὸν ὡς <u>κύνα</u>[8] ὃν
ἐξέβαλον οἱ ἄνθρωποι ἀπὸ προσώπου αὐτῶν καὶ
ἔξω τῆς οἰκίας τηροῦσιν, ὅτι κακὸς ἦν καὶ <u>ἔδακνεν</u>[9]
αὐτούς."

---

6 μισέω 'I hate'

7 ἐκκλίνω 'I turn aside'

8 κύων, κυνός, ὁ 'dog'

9 δάκνω 'I bite'

27. The Contest

Ἀδελφὸς μένων ἐν τοῖς Μονιδίοις <u>πολλάκις</u>[1]
ἔπιπτεν εἰς <u>πορνείαν</u>[2]· καὶ οὐκ <u>ἐνεκάκει</u>[3], ἀλλὰ
πολλὰ προσευχόμενος μᾶλλον παρεκάλει τὸν Θεὸν
καὶ <u>ἔκλαιε</u>[4] λέγων· "Κύριε, κἂν θέλω κἂν μὴ θέλω,
σῶσόν με. ὅτι ἐγὼ ὁ πονηρὸς οὐ δύναμαι ἀφῆσαι τὴν
<u>πορνείαν</u>, ἀλλὰ σὺ ὡς Θεὸς δύνασαί με τηρεῖν ἀπὸ
τῆς ἁμαρτίας. ἐὰν γὰρ τὸν δίκαιον <u>ἐλεήσῃς</u>[5], οὐδὲν
μέγα· καὶ ἐὰν τὸν ἀγαθὸν σώσῃς, τίς <u>θαυμάσει</u>[6];
καλὸν γάρ ἐστιν τὸ καλοὺς <u>ἐλεεῖν</u>. ἐμέ δέ, Κύριε, τὸν
<u>ἁμαρτωλὸν</u>[7] <u>ἐλέησον</u>, ἵνα εἴδω τὴν ἀγάπην σου· ὅτι
<u>σοὶ ἐγκαταλέλειπται</u>[8] ὁ <u>πτωχός</u>[9]." ταῦτα οὖν ἔλεγε
καθ᾽ ἡμέραν, ἢ ἔπιπτεν ἢ οὐκ ἔπιπτεν. πεσὼν δέ ποτε
εἰς τὴν <u>πορνείαν</u> νυκτός, ἀνέστη εὐθὺς καὶ ἤρξατο
προσεύχεσθαι. ὁ δὲ Διάβολος <u>θαυμάσας</u> τὴν ἐλπίδα
καὶ τὴν <u>παρρησίαν</u>[10] αὐτοῦ πρὸς τὸν Θεόν, ἀνέβη
ἐνώπιον αὐτοῦ καὶ λέγει· "ὅταν προσεύχῃ, πῶς οὐκ
<u>ἐντρέπῃ</u>[11] ὅλως στῆναι ἐνώπιον τοῦ Θεοῦ ἢ καλέσαι
τὸ ὄνομα αὐτοῦ;" λέγει αὐτῷ ὁ ἀδελφός· "ὁ τόπος

---

1 πολλάκις 'often'

2 πορνεία, -ας, ἡ 'fornication'

3 ἐνκακέω 'I give up'

4 κλαίω 'I cry'

5 ἐλεέω 'I have mercy'

6 θαυμάζω 'I wonder at'

7 ἁμαρτωλός, -ή, -όν 'sinful'

8 ἐγκαταλείπω 'I leave, forsake'

9 πτωχός, -οῦ, ὁ 'poor'

10 παρρησία, -ας, ἡ 'boldness'

11 ἐντρέπομαι 'I am ashamed'

οὗτος <u>στάδιόν</u>[12] ἐστιν καὶ ἡμεῖς <u>πυκτεύομεν</u>[13] μεθ᾽
ἀλλήλων· σοῦ μὲν διδόντος ποτέ ἐγὼ λαμβάνω,
ἐμοῦ δὲ πάλιν διδόντος σὺ λαμβάνεις. ἀλλὰ γίνωσκε
ὅτι ἕως θανάτου πρὸς σὲ <u>πυκτεύω</u> ἢ ἕως ἂν ἔλθῃ
ἡ ἐσχάτη ἡμέρα. καὶ μαρτυρῶ σοι—ὁ γὰρ Κύριός
μου ἦλθεν σῶσαι <u>*ἁμαρτωλοὺς*</u> *εἰς* <u>*μετάνοιαν*</u>[14]—ὅτι
οὐ μὴ <u>παύσωμαι</u>[15] κατὰ σοῦ προσευχόμενος τῷ
Θεῷ, ἕως οὗ <u>παύσῃ</u> καὶ σὺ <u>πυκτεύων</u> πρός με. καὶ
ἴδωμεν τίς τὸν <u>στέφανον</u>[16] λήμψεται, σὺ ἢ ὁ Θεός;"
ταῦτα ἀκούσας τὸ δαιμόνιον λέγει αὐτῷ· "καὶ ἐπ᾽
ἀληθείας λοιπὸν οὐκέτι <u>πυκτεύω</u> πρός σε, ἵνα μὴ διὰ
τὴν πίστιν σου <u>στέφανον</u> λάβῃς." καὶ ἀπῆλθεν ἀπ᾽
αὐτοῦ τὸ δαιμόνιον καὶ ἀπέλυσεν αὐτὸν ἀπὸ τῆς
ἡμέρας ἐκείνης. ἰδοὺ τί ἀγαθόν ἐστιν ἡ ἐλπὶς καὶ τὸ
μὴ <u>ἐγκακεῖν</u> καὶ <u>παρρησίαν</u> ἔχειν ἐνώπιον Θεοῦ, εἰ
καὶ γίνηται <u>πολλάκις</u> <u>πυκτεύειν</u> ἡμᾶς ἐν τῷ <u>σταδίῳ</u>
καὶ πεσεῖν ποτε εἰς ἁμαρτίας. ἐλθόντος οὖν τοῦ
ἀδελφοῦ εἰς <u>μετάνοιαν</u>, τοῦ λοιποῦ ἐκάθητο <u>κλαίων</u>
τὰς ἁμαρτίας αὐτοῦ. ὅτε οὖν ἔλεγεν αὐτῷ ἡ ψυχὴ ὅτι·
"καλῶς ποιεῖς <u>κλαίων</u>," ἔλεγε καὶ αὐτὸς τῇ ψυχῇ· "τί
τοῦτο λέγεις καλόν; τί γὰρ θέλει ὁ Θεός, ἵνα *ἀπολέσῃ*
τις τὴν ψυχήν αὐτοῦ καὶ κάθηται <u>κλαίων</u> αὐτὴν; οὐ,
ἀλλὰ θέλω ἵνα σωθῇ ἡ ψυχή μου."

---

12 στάδιον, -ου, τό 'arena; stadium'

13 πυκτεύω 'I fight; box'

14 μετάνοια, -ας, ἡ 'repentance'

15 παύομαι 'I stop, cease'

16 στέφανος, -ου, ὁ '(victor's) crown'

28. Do Not Judge

Πρεσβύτερός τις ἐκάθητο μέγας ἐν τῷ ὄρει τῆς
Συρίας. εἶχε δὲ ἀδελφὸν <u>ταχὺν</u>[1] εἰς τὸ κρῖναι ὅταν
ἔβλεπε τινὰ κακόν τι ποιῶντα. <u>πολλάκις</u>[2] οὖν
παρεκάλει αὐτὸν ὁ πρεσβύτερος περὶ τούτου λέγων·
'πολύ, τέκνον, <u>πλανᾶσαι</u>[3] καὶ μόνος ἀπολλύεις
σου τὴν ψυχήν. *οὐδεὶς γὰρ οἶδε τὰ τοῦ ἀνθρώπου, εἰ
μὴ τὸ πνεῦμα τὸ ἐν αὐτῷ.* καὶ γὰρ πολλοὶ <u>πολλάκις</u>
ἐνώπιον ἀνθρώπων πολλὰ κακὰ ποιοῦσιν, κατ᾽ ἰδίαν
δὲ <u>ἐν κρυπτῷ</u>[4] τῷ Θεῷ <u>μετενόησαν</u>[5]· καὶ τὴν μὲν
ἁμαρτίαν ἡμεῖς εἴδομεν, τὰ δὲ ἀγαθὰ ἃ ἐποίει μόνος
ὁ Θεὸς γινώσκει. καὶ γὰρ πολλοὶ πᾶσαν τὴν ζωὴν
αὐτῶν κακῶς ζήσαντες <u>πολλάκις</u> περὶ τὸν θάνατον
αὐτῶν εἰς <u>μετάνοιαν</u>[6] εὑρεθέντες ἐσώθησαν· εἰσὶ καὶ
ἄνθρωποι πολλὰς ἁμαρτίας ἔχοντες, οἳ ἐδέχθησαν ὅτι
ἅγιοι ἄνθρωποι ὑπὲρ αὐτῶν προσηύξαντο. διὰ τοῦτο
<u>κἂν</u> αὐτοῖς τοῖς ὀφθαλμοῖς αὐτοῦ ἴδῃ ἄνθρωπος, μὴ
κρινέτω τὸν ἀδελφὸν αὐτοῦ· εἷς ἔστιν ὁ <u>κριτής</u>[7],
ὁ υἱὸς τοῦ Θεοῦ. πᾶς δὲ ἄνθρωπος ὁ κρίνων τινὰ
<u>ἀντίχριστον</u>[8] ἑαυτὸν ποιεῖ· ὅτι τὴν δόξαν καὶ τὴν
ἐξουσίαν, ἣν ἔδωκεν αὐτῷ ὁ πατήρ, ἔλαβε <u>κριτὴς</u>
γενόμενος.'

---

1 ταχύς, -εῖα, -ύ 'fast, swift'

2 πολλάκις 'often'

3 πλανάομαι 'I am deceived'

4 ἐν κρυπτῷ 'in secret'

5 μετανοέω 'I repent'

6 μετάνοια, -ας, ἡ 'repentance'

7 κριτής, -οῦ, ὁ 'judge'

8 ἀντίχριστος, -ου, ὁ 'rival of Christ; antichrist'

29. Woe to That Sinner

For the Desert Fathers, an 'antichrist' was one who put himself 'in the place of Christ' by judging his brother. Here a single judgmental word costs Abba John of Saba his monastic habit, the sign of his office.

Ὁ μέγας Ἰωάννης ὁ Σαβαΐτης ἔλεγεν· "καθεζομένου μου ποτέ," φησίν, "ἐν τῇ <u>ἐρήμῳ</u>⁹ προσῆλθέ μοι ἀδελφός τις. ἠρώτων οὖν αὐτὸν πῶς ἔχουσιν οἱ πατέρες καὶ ἔλεγέ μοι· 'σοῦ ὑπὲρ αὐτῶν προσευχομένου, καλῶς.' ἠρώτησα οὖν αὐτὸν περὶ ἀδελφοῦ τινος πονηροῦ καὶ ὄνομα ἔχοντος κακόν. καὶ λέγει μοι καὶ αὐτός· 'γίνωσκε, πάτερ, ὅτι ἐκεῖνος ὁ πονηρὸς ἔτι ὁ αὐτός ἐστιν.' τοῦτο οὖν ἀκούσας ἐγὼ εἶπον· '<u>οὐαὶ</u>¹⁰ τῷ <u>ἁμαρτωλῷ</u>¹¹.' καὶ ὡς εἶπα τὸ 'οὐαί', εὐθὺς φέρομαι ὡς ἐν <u>ὁράσει</u>¹² καὶ θεωρῶ ἐμαυτὸν ἐνώπιον τοῦ Γολγοθᾶ ἱστάμενον. καὶ ἰδοὺ ὁ Κύριος ἡμῶν Ἰησοῦς Χριστὸς ἐν μέσῳ τῶν δύο <u>λῃστῶν</u>¹³ ἐπὶ τοῦ <u>σταυροῦ</u>¹⁴. ἀναστὰς οὖν προσῆλθον αὐτῷ προσκυνῆσαι καὶ ἔπεσον ἐπὶ πρόσωπον παρὰ τοὺς πόδας αὐτοῦ. ὡς δὲ τοῦτο εἶδεν, ἐκάλεσε μεγάλῃ τῇ φωνῇ τοῖς ἁγίοις ἀγγέλοις αὐτοῦ λέγων· 'βάλλετε

---

9 ἔρημος, -ου, ἡ 'desert'

10 οὐαί 'woe, alas'

11 ἁμαρτωλός, -ή, -όν 'sinful'

12 ὅρασις, -εως, ἡ 'vision'

13 λῃστής, -οῦ, ὁ 'robber; rebel'

14 σταυρός, -οῦ, ὁ 'cross'

αὐτὸν ἔξω, ὅτι <u>ἀντίχριστός</u>[1] μου ἐστί. <u>πρὸ</u>[2] τοῦ γὰρ
ἐμὲ κρῖναι, αὐτὸς ἤδη ἔκρινε τὸν ἀδελφὸν αὐτοῦ.'
ἀκούσας δὲ ἐφοβήθην καὶ εὐθὺς ἀπῆλθον ἀπὸ
προσώπου αὐτοῦ. οἱ δὲ ἄγγελοι ἀκολουθήσαντες
ἔλαβόν μου τὸ ἱμάτιον καὶ ἐξέβαλόν με ἔξω. καὶ
εὐθὺς εἰς ἐμαυτὸν ἐγενόμην καὶ λέγω τῷ ἄλλῳ
ἀδελφῷ· 'πονηρὰ ἡ ἡμέρα αὕτη ἐμοί.' καὶ λέγει μοι·
'διὰ τί, πάτερ;' καὶ τότε ἔλεγον αὐτῷ τὴν <u>ὅρασίν</u>
μου καὶ εἶπα· 'τὸ ἱμάτιόν μου σημεῖόν ἐστιν παρὰ
τοῦ Κυρίου τοῦ εἶναί με ἄνθρωπον Θεοῦ. καὶ ἰδοὺ
ἦρεν αὐτὸ ἀπό μου καὶ ἔβαλέν με ἔξω.' καὶ ἐκ τῆς
ἡμέρας ἐκείνης ἑπτὰ <u>ἔτη</u>[3] ἐποίησα <u>πλανώμενος</u>[4] ἐν τῇ
ἐρήμῳ· οὔτε ἄρτον ἤσθιον, οὔτε εἰς οἶκον εἰσηρχόμην,
οὔτε ἄνθρωπον ἔβλεπον. μετὰ δὲ τὸν πολὺν τοῦτον
χρόνον, πάλιν <u>ἐφάνη</u>[5] μοι ὁ Κύριος ἐπὶ τοῦ <u>σταυροῦ</u>
καθὼς καὶ τὸ πρότερον. καὶ ἀφῆκεν τοὺς ἀγγέλους
αὐτοῦ ἀποδοῦναί μοι τὸ ἱμάτιόν μου.' ἡμεῖς δὲ ταῦτα
περὶ τοῦ μακαρίου Ἰωάννου ἀκούσαντες εἴπομεν ὅτι·
'εἰ ὁ δίκαιος <u>μόλις</u>[6] σώζεται, ὁ <u>ἀσεβὴς</u>[7] καὶ <u>ἁμαρτωλὸς</u>
<u>ποῦ</u>[8] <u>φανεῖται;</u>'''

---

1 ἀντίχριστος, -ου, ὁ 'rival of Christ; antichrist'

2 πρό 'before'

3 ἔτος, -ους, τό 'year'

4 πλανάομαι 'I wander; err; am deceived'

5 φαίνομαι 'I appear'

6 μόλις 'hardly'

7 ἀσεβής, -ές 'ungodly'

8 ποῦ 'where'

30. *Abba Macarius and Wine*

Ἔλεγον περὶ τοῦ ἀββᾶ Μακαρίου ὅτι ὅταν μετὰ
ἀδελφῶν ἦν, ἐτίθει ἑαυτῷ νόμον· ʽἐὰν ᾖ οἶνος⁹, διὰ
τοὺς ἀδελφοὺς πίνε. καὶ ἀντὶ¹⁰ ἑνὸς ποτηρίου¹¹
οἴνου, μίαν ἡμέραν μὴ πίῃς ὕδωρ.ʼ οἱ οὖν ἀδελφοὶ μὴ
εἰδόντες τὶ ἐποίει, ἐδίδουν αὐτῷ ποτήρια πολλά. ὁ
δὲ πρεσβύτερος μετὰ χαρᾶς ἐλάμβανεν, ἵνα μὴ χαρῇ
ἡ σάρξ αὐτοῦ. ὁ δὲ μαθητὴς αὐτοῦ εἰδὼς τί γίνεται,
ἔλεγε τοῖς ἀδελφοῖς· ʽμὴ γένοιτο, ἀδελφοί, μὴ δῶτε
αὐτῷ πλεῖον· εἰ δὲ μή, ἐν τῷ οἴκῳ αὐτοῦ μέλλει
ἑαυτὸν ἀποκτεῖναι ὕδωρ μὴ πίνων.ʼ καὶ ἀκούσαντες οἱ
ἀδελφοί, οὐκέτι¹² αὐτῷ ἐδίδουν.

---

9 οἶνος, -ου, ὁ ʽwineʼ

10 ἀντί ʽin exchange for; againstʼ

11 ποτήριον, -ου, τό ʽcupʼ

12 οὐκέτι ʽno moreʼ

31. Go and Revile the Dead

Ἀδελφὸς προσῆλθε τῷ ἀββᾷ Μακαρίῳ τῷ Αἰγυπτίῳ, καὶ λέγει αὐτῷ· 'ἀββᾶ, εἰπέ μοι ῥῆμα· πῶς σωθῶ;' καὶ λέγει ὁ πρεσβύτερος· 'ὕπαγε εἰς τὰ μνημεῖα[1] καὶ ὕβρισον[2] τοὺς νεκρούς.' ἀπελθὼν οὖν ὁ ἀδελφὸς, ὕβρισε καὶ λίθους ἐπ' αὐτοὺς ἔβαλεν· καὶ ἐλθὼν εἶπε τῷ πρεσβυτέρῳ ὃ ἐποίησεν. καὶ λέγει αὐτῷ· 'οὐδέν σοι ἐλάλησαν;' ὁ δὲ ἔφη· 'οὐχί.' λέγει αὐτῷ ὁ πρεσβύτερος· 'ὕπαγε πάλιν καὶ εὐλόγησον[3] αὐτούς.' ἀπελθὼν οὖν ὁ ἀδελφὸς ηὐλόγησεν αὐτοὺς λέγων· 'ἀπόστολοι, ἅγιοι, καὶ δίκαιοι.' καὶ ἦλθε πρὸς τὸν πρεσβύτερον καὶ εἶπεν αὐτῷ· 'ηὐλόγησα.' καὶ λέγει αὐτῷ· 'οὐδέν σοι ἀπεκρίθησαν;' ἔφη ὁ ἀδελφός· 'οὐχί.' λέγει αὐτῷ ὁ πρεσβύτερος· 'οἶδας πῶς ὕβρισας αὐτοὺς καὶ οὐδέν σοι ἀπεκρίθησαν; καὶ πῶς ηὐλόγησας αὐτοὺς καὶ οὐδέν σοι ἐλάλησαν; οὕτως καὶ σύ, ἐὰν θέλῃς σωθῆναι, γενοῦ[4] νεκρός· μή σοι μέλῃ[5] περὶ τῆς ἀδικίας[6] τῶν ἀνθρώπων, μηδὲ περὶ τῆς δόξης αὐτῶν, καθὼς καὶ τοῖς νεκροῖς οὐ μέλει περὶ τούτων· καὶ οὕτως δύνασαι σωθῆναι.'

---

1 μνημεῖον, -ου, τό 'tomb'

2 ὑβρίζω 'I insult, mistreat'

3 εὐλογέω 'I bless'

4 γενοῦ 'become' (masc. sing. pres. impv. γίνομαι 'I become, happen')

5 μή σοι μέλῃ 'do not care about' (impers. pres. act. subj. μέλει 'there is care')

6 ἀδικία, -ας, ἡ 'injustice'

32. My Sins Fall to the Ground

Ἀδελφός τις ἔπεσέ ποτε εἰς ἁμαρτίαν ἐν τῇ Σκήτει·
καὶ γενομένου <u>συνεδρίου</u>⁷, ἵνα κρίνωσι τί αὐτῷ
ποιήσωσιν, ἀπέστειλαν πρὸς τὸν ἀββᾶν Μωϋσέα.
ὁ δὲ οὐκ ἤθελεν ἐλθεῖν. ἀπέστειλαν οὖν πάλιν
πρὸς αὐτὸν οἱ πρεσβύτεροι λέγοντες· ʽἐλθέ· ὁ γὰρ
λαός σε <u>περιμένει</u>⁸.ʾ ὁ δὲ ἀναστὰς ἦλθε. καὶ λαβὼν
<u>σπυρίδα</u>⁹ ἔβαλεν εἰς αὐτὴν ὕδωρ καὶ <u>ἤνεγκεν</u>¹⁰ εἰς
τὸ <u>συνέδριον</u> (ὡς δὲ περιεπάτει, <u>ἐξεχύνετο</u>¹¹ πάλιν
τὸ ὕδωρ ἐκ τῆς <u>σπυρίδος</u> καὶ ἔπιπτε ἐπὶ τὴν γῆν). οἱ
δὲ ἀδελφοὶ ἐξελθόντες πρὸς αὐτὸν λέγουσιν αὐτῷ·
ʽτί ἐστι τοῦτο, πάτερ;ʾ εἶπε δὲ αὐτοῖς ὁ πρεσβύτερος·
ʽἰδοὺ αἱ ἁμαρτίαι μου αἱ πολλαὶ <u>ὀπίσω</u>¹² μου ἐπὶ τὴν
γῆν πίπτουσι, καὶ οὐ βλέπω αὐτάς· καὶ νῦν ἦλθον
ἵνα τὰς ἁμαρτίας τοῦ ἀδελφοῦ μου κρίνω.ʾ οἱ δὲ
ἀκούσαντες, οὐδὲν ἐλάλησαν τῷ ἀδελφῷ, ἀλλὰ
ἀπέλυσαν αὐτόν.

---

7 συνέδριον, -ου, τό ʽcouncil; Sanhedrinʾ

8 περιμένω ʽI wait forʾ

9 σπυρίς, -ίδος, ἡ ʽbasketʾ

10 ἤνεγκεν ʽbroughtʾ (3 per. sing. aor. act. ind. φέρω ʽI carryʾ)

11 ἐκχέω ʽI spill, pour out; shed (blood)ʾ

12 ὀπίσω ʽbehindʾ

English Translations

The translations in this section are rendered in idiomatic English, so that the student can get a feel for how the vocabulary is actually used in context.

1. How to Pray

One of the brothers came to a certain elder who was staying at Mount Sinai and implored him, saying, "Father, tell me how I ought to pray, for I have many sins before God." The elder said to him, "My child, whenever I pray, I speak like this: 'Lord, I want to serve You as I served Satan and love You as I loved sin.'"

2. The Watchful Father

Once we were at Raithu, and the brothers told us
that there was a great elder who lived (καθήμενος)
in the hill country (ἐν τῷ ὄρει) of the land of Israel.
And this elder guarded his spirit so much (οὕτως)
that he would not even walk without praying first (εἰ
μὴ πρῶτον προσηύξατο). Then, after going a little
ways and stopping, he would pray again and examine
himself, saying, "How are we (πῶς ἔχομεν), brother? What are you doing?" And if he found his spirit
glorifying God or praying, then all was well (καλῶς);
but if he found himself doing anything else, he would
rebuke himself at once, saying, "Come here, you fool,
and return to your work (πάλιν εἰς τὸ ἔργον σου)."
And he would do this multiple times wherever he
walked. And every day the elder would say to himself,
"Brother, the hour of your departure is near, and you
have done nothing." Once Satan came to him and
said, "Why do you still labor? For there is no hope for
you to be saved." But he replied to him, "And even if
I am not saved, then at least I will be found standing
over your head, and you will be last of all in Gehen-
na."

3. The Fallen Pillar

Abba Anthony heard about a certain other father who had done a miracle (σημεῖον) on the road. For he had seen some elders who had been travelling for a long time (πολὺν χρόνον ἤδη) on the road and could not go any further (ἔτι). So he spoke to the beasts and told them to carry the elders until they reached Anthony. And the elders then told this to Abba Anthony. And he said to them, "This father seems to me to be a boat bearing many goods; but I do not know if it will reach the harbor safely (ἐν εἰρήνῃ)." And after some time Abba Anthony suddenly began to weep and cry out with a loud voice. His disciples said to him, "Why are you weeping, Abba?" And the elder said, "A great pillar of the church has just (νῦν) fallen,"—now he was speaking about the other father—"go now," he said, "to him and see what has happened." So the disciples left and found the father sitting on the ground, and weeping over the sin he had committed. And when he saw the disciples of Abba Anthony, he said, "Tell the father, 'Father, beseech God on my behalf, that he might give me just seven days, that I might repent.'" But after only three days, he died.

4. The Right Answer

Once fathers came to Abba Anthony, and Abba Joseph was with them. Now, the elder wished to test them, so he asked them about a certain difficult passage (ῥήματος) from Scripture. And he began to question them from the least (ἐσχάτων) to the greatest, saying, "What is this word? What does this mean (τί θέλει τοῦτο λέγειν)?" And each answered according to his ability. And Abba Anthony would say to each of them, "You have not yet found it. You have answered wrongly (οὐ καλῶς εἶπας)." Then, last of all, he said to Abba Joseph, "And what do you say this passage means (πῶς εἶναι)?" He replied, "I do not know." And Abba Anthony said, "Abba Joseph has found the way, for he has said, 'I do not know.'"

5. *Steal the Donkey*

Brothers came from Scetis to Abba Anthony. And as they were going down to the sea to journey to him, they found an elder who also (καὶ αὐτόν) wished to go there (now, the brothers did not know who the elder was). And as they sat in the boat, they spoke about (ἐλάλουν λόγους) the church fathers, and Scripture, and again concerning their own handi-work. The elder, however (δέ), was silent. And when they reached land, the elder was also found to be going to Abba Anthony. When they reached him, Anthony said to them, "You have found a good brother, this elder." And he said to the elder as well, "You have found good brothers to travel with (μετὰ σοῦ), Abba." And the elder replied, "Yes (μέν), they are good, but their house has no door, and whoever wants to (πᾶς ὁ θέλων) can enter in and untie the donkey." He said this because they spoke whatever (πάντα) came into their mouths.

6. *Wild Men of the Desert*

Once Macarius the Egyptian went from Scetis to the mountains (εἰς τὸ ὄρος) of Nitria to worship God together with Abba Pambo. The elders said to him, "Speak a word to the brothers, O man of God." He said, "I am not yet (οὔπω γέγονα) a man of God, but I have seen men of God. Once, when I was sitting in my house in Scetis I heard the voice of my soul saying, 'Go out into the desert, and see what you can see there.' I remained in doubt concerning this for many years, saying, 'What if (μὴ) it comes from the demons?' But when my soul would not stop saying this, but insisted (παρεκάλει) all the more, I went out into the desert. And there I found a sea of water, and an island in the midst of it. And the beasts of the desert came to drink from it, and I saw among them two naked men, and I was afraid, for I thought that they were spirits. But when they saw that I was afraid, they said to me. 'Fear not, we too are men.' And I said to them, 'Where are you from and how did you come to this desert?' And they said, 'We used to live (ἐζήσαμέν ποτε) together with many brothers, and we agreed to come out here; and it has been forty years since then (ἰδού). One of us is an Egyptian, the other is a Libyan.' And they in turn (καὶ αὐτοί) asked me, saying, 'How is (πῶς ἔχει) the world? Does the water still come in its season, and is the world at peace (ἔχει τὴν εἰρήνην αὐτοῦ)?' And I answered them, 'Yes.' And then I asked them, 'How can I become a man of God?' And they told me, 'Unless (ἐὰν μή) one forsakes everything in the world, he cannot become a man of God.'

And I said to them, 'But I am a child, and I cannot be like you.' And they in turn replied to me, 'Well if you cannot be like us, then sit in your house and pray over your sins.' And I asked them, 'When winter comes (γίνηται), are you not troubled (κακῶς ἔχετε)? And when summer comes, does not your flesh perish?' But they replied, 'God has given (ἐποίησεν) us this grace, that our bodies can bear both the cold in winter and the heat in summer.' And that is why I told you that I am not yet a man of God, but I have seen such men."

7. Three Visions

Abba Daniel said, 'Abba Arsenius told us this story as if it were about someone else (but it was Abba Arsenius himself who did it). Once a certain elder was sitting in his house, when a voice came to him, saying: 'Come, and I will show you the works of men.' And he got up and went out. And the Spirit led him to a certain place and showed him a man chopping wood. And the man collected them together (ἐπὶ τὸ αὐτό) and made a great pile (φορτίον). And he wanted to lift it, but he was not able. But he did not take wood from the pile so that he could lift it, but rather chopped more (ἄλλα) wood and threw it on the pile. And this he did many times, and the pile grew larger. And going on a little, he showed him a man standing at a well of water. And he carried water out of it and poured (ἔβαλεν) it into a cracked vessel. And the same water went into the vessel and back out again into the well. And the voice said to him again, 'Come, and I will show you another.' And he saw a temple and two men sitting on horses before it. And the two were carrying a great beam (ξύλον), like a yoke, between them. And they wanted to enter into the temple, but could not, because the beam was between them. And nether wanted to humble himself and dismount from the horse to follow the other and carry the beam straight forward (ἐπ᾽ εὐθείας). And for that reason they remained outside of the temple. 'These,' he said, 'are those who carry the yoke of righteousness, and think highly of themselves in their glory. And they do not humble themselves to repent and go in the way of Christ. And that is why they remain outside of the kingdom of God. And the one who is chopping the wood is a man in many sins. And yet he does not repent, but throws yet other evils onto the sins he had at first (πρώτας ἁμαρτίας). And the one carrying the water is a man who does good works, but has among them evil works as well. And therefore he has lost his good works together with them.' Therefore, every man must attend to his works, that he might not perish."

8. Sunday Worship

Again, they said of Abba Arsenius that on Saturdays he would stand all night until the light of day would come again. And leaving the light behind him, he would stretch out his hands to heaven in prayer, until the light would fall on his face again. And thus having spent the whole day in prayer (προσευξάμενος), he would sit down.

9. *The Power of Sight*

They said of one of the great fathers that he lived (καθήμενος) on Mount Porphyry, and when he would lift his eyes to heaven he would see all things in heaven, and when he looked into the earth he would see the abyss and all that was in it.

10. *The Destruction of Scetis*

They said of one of the great elders of Scetis that whenever someone left the world wishing to stay with the brothers, the other brothers would build him a house. And this elder would come out with great joy and be the first to lay (πρῶτος θήσας) the foundation and would not leave until the work had been completed. Now, once when he was coming out to build a house, he was not joyful but very sorrowful. And the brothers said to him, "Why are you sorrowful, Abba?" He said, "This place is going (μέλλει) to be destroyed, my children. For I have seen that a great fire arose in Scetis. And the brothers took water and garments and made every effort (πάντα ἐποίουν) to quench it. And again a fire rose up and again they quenched it. And it happened a third time, and filled all of Scetis, and nothing could be saved. That is why I am sorrowful."

11. The Insistent Beggar

Once Abba Agatho went into the city to sell his baskets and found a lame man by the road. The lame man said to him, "Where are you going?" And Abba Agatho said to him, "To the city to sell baskets." And he said to him, "Sir, take me there." And he brought him to the city. And he said to him, "Put me where you are selling baskets." And he did so. And when he had sold one basket, the lame man said to him, "How much did you sell it for?" And he said, "This much." And he said to him, "Buy me bread." And he bought it. And again he sold another basket. And he said, "And how much for this one?" And he said, "This much." And he said to him, "Buy me that." And he bought it. And after he had sold all his baskets, Abba Agatho wanted to depart. And the lame man said to him. "Are you going?" And he said to him, "The time has come." And he said, "Sir, if you can, take me back (πάλιν) to where you found me." And he took him to his place. And he said to him, "You have favor (χάριν), Agatho, with the Lord in heaven and on earth." And he lifted up his eyes and saw no one, for it was an angel of the Lord who had come to see his love.

12. The Forgetful Father

There was a certain elder at Scetis in Egypt. His body was very strong (μεγάλην εἶχεν δύναμιν), but not his spirit; he could not remember anything, but forgot everything. One time he went to see Abba John, to ask him about memory. And after hearing a word from him, he returned to his home, and immediately forgot what Abba John had said to him. And he went again to ask him, and after hearing the same word from him again, he returned again. But when he reached his own home, he had forgotten again. And thus he went many times, but when he returned he could not remember the word. So after this he went to Abba John and said, "You know, Abba, I forgot what you had told me again, but I did not come back so as not to annoy you." Abba John said to him, "Go and light a lamp." And he lit one. And he said to him again, "Bring other lamps and light them from this one." And he did so. And Abba John said to the elder, "Now (μὴ τί ποτε), did you annoy the lamp when you lit the other lamps from it?" He said, "Not at all (οὐχί)." And the Abba said, "And John is not annoyed either (οὐδὲ Ἰωάννης). If all of Scetis should come to me, it would by no means remove me from the grace of Christ. So come whenever you wish, and do not fear." And thus through the love of the two men, God granted the father the power of memory. And this was the work of the Scetiotes, to give grace to those who have none and to instruct one another in goodness.

13. The Ship at Sea

It once happened that a certain brother fell into sin, while he was staying with the disciples of Abba Elit. The other brothers cast him out into the desert. So he travelled and went to the mountain where Abba Anthony was (εἰς τὸ ὄρος πρὸς τὸν ἀββᾶν Ἀντώνιον). And after the brother had stayed with him for a long time, Abba Anthony sent him back to his brothers. But when they saw him, they did not welcome him, but cast him out again. So he went to Abba Anthony, saying, "They did not want to receive me, father." And the elder sent him saying, "Tell them this parable: 'A boat was being tormented in the sea, and lost all the goods that were in it, and it itself barely escaped (ἐσώθη) onto the land. But you want to cast what has escaped (τὰ σωθέντα) back out again into the sea.'" And when they heard that Abba Anthony had sent him, they received him at once.

14. Doers, Not Hearers

Abba Eulogius, son of Enatus (ὁ τοῦ Ἐνάτου), said that a certain brother lived in Cellia, who did nothing but (οὐδὲν εἰ μή) read, night and day. One day he got up and gathered all the books he had and gave them to the other brothers. And taking his garment, he went out into the desert. Abba Isaac went to him and said, "Where are you going, my child?" And the brother responded, "Behold, father, I do nothing night and day but listen to the words of books. Now I want to begin to practice in deeds what I have heard from the books." And so he released him, after praying over him.

15. Forgive Us Our Debts

Once a certain brother came to Abba Silvanus to the mountains of Panepho and said to him, "Abba, I have an enemy who has done me much harm (πολλὰ κακά). He even threw me out of my home when I was still in the world and sought (ἤθελε) to destroy me all the time. And now I want to hand him over to the magistrate so that he can avenge me." And the elder said, "Do according to your will, my child." And the brother said, "Yes, Abba, and if he suffers thus, then his soul will more likely (μᾶλλον) be saved." And the elder said, "Do as it seems right to you (καθὼς δοκεῖ σοι), my child." And the brother said to the elder, "Arise, father, and let us pray, and then I will go to the magistrate." And the elder arose, and while they were saying the "Our Father", when they were about to say, "And forgive us our trespasses as we forgive those who trespass against us," the elder said, "as we *do not* forgive those who trespass against us." And the brother said to the elder, "Not like that, father." And the elder said, "How then (ἀλλὰ πῶς), my child? For if you want to go to the magistrate for him to avenge you, then Silvanus will certainly not pray for you." And so the brother repented and forgave his enemy.

16. The Tax Collector and the Corpse

One of the fathers said that there was once a tax collector who had been sent by the emperor (βασιλέως).
And on the way he found a dead man lying naked
on the ground. And when he saw him, he said to his
servant, "Take the horse and go on a little ways." And
so the tax collector got down from the horse, took
his fine (καλόν) garment, threw it over the naked
body, and left. A few days later, the same tax collector
was sent to another country. And it happened that
as he was leaving the city, he fell from his horse and
broke his foot. His servant carried him to his home
and called the doctors. After a few days, his foot had
turned (ἐγένετο) black. And when the doctors saw
that his foot had turned black, they said to themselves privately (κατ' ἰδίαν) that the foot needed to
be amputated (ἐκκοπῆναι). Otherwise (εἰ δὲ μή), it
would infect the whole body (πονηρὸν μέλλει ποιεῖν)
and the man would die. So they said to him, "We
will come in the morning and tell you what we think
about your situation (τὰ περί σου)." The tax collector
told his servant to follow after the doctors and ascer-
tain the truth from them. And they told him, "Your
master's foot has turned black, and unless it is cut off,
the man will perish. We will come in the morning
and do as God wills." So the servant came in to his
master with sorrow (λυπούμενος) and said, "This is
what they think concerning you." And when he heard
it, he was distressed and so sorrowful that he could
not sleep. Now, there was a little light still burning in
the house. Around midnight, he saw a man coming

toward him and saying to him, "Why are you sorrowful? Why are you distressed?" And he said, "Sir, do
you not want me to be sorrowful and distressed, when
I have been broken, and the doctors are saying such
things about me?" And the one who had appeared to
him said, "Let me see your foot." And he anointed it
and said, "Get up now and walk." And the tax collector
said, "It is broken; I cannot." And he said to him, "Take
(κράτησον) my hand." And so he took it and walked a
little. And the one who had appeared to him said, "You
still cannot walk normally (καλῶς)? Sit back down so
I can see your foot. And again he anointed his other
foot. And he said to him, "Get up now and walk." And
so he got up and walked normally. And he said to him,
"Sit back down." And he spoke some words to him
about mercy, that the Lord had spoken: *"Blessed are
the merciful, for they shall obtain mercy* (Matt 5:7); *but
judgment is without mercy to the one who has shown no
mercy* (Jas 2:13)," and other such things. And he said
to him, "Farewell (χαῖρε)." And the tax collector said,
"Are you going?" And he answered him, "What else (τί
ἔτι) do you want? You are now healthy (καλῶς ἔχεις)."
And the tax collector said to him, "Tell me who you
are; for I know that God has sent you." And he said to
him, "Look at me. Do you not recognize this garment?"
And he said to him, "Yes, sir, it is mine." And the man
said to him, "I am the one you saw dead lying in the
road, and you threw your garment over me. And God
has sent me to you. Therefore give thanks (ἔχε χάριν) to
God forever (εἰς τὸν αἰῶνα)." And he left again just as
he had come. And the tax collector glorified God, from
whom every good thing comes down.

17. The Dead Man's Pledge

Abba Sisoes said, "When I was at Scetis with Macarius, we went out to harvest with him, seven people (ὀνόματα). And behold, a widow was gleaning (συνάγουσα) after us, and she would not stop weeping. So Macarius called the master of the field and said to him, "What is the matter with that woman (τί ἔχει ἡ γυνή αὕτη), for she will not stop weeping?" And he said to him, "Her husband had taken a pledge from someone, and died suddenly without telling (καὶ οὐκ εἶπεν) anyone where he had put it when he died. And now the owner (κύριος) of the pledge wants to take her and her children as slaves." The elder said to him, 'Tell her to come to us where we are resting during the noonday heat (τὸ καῦμα).' And when the woman had come, the elder said to her, 'Woman, why (τί) do you not stop weeping like this?" And she said, "My husband died after taking a pledge from someone and did not say where he had hidden it before he died." And the father said to her, "Come, take (ἄγε) us to where you have put your husband.' And so she took the brothers along, and they went with her. And when they came to the place, the elder said to her, "Go to your house." And when they had prayed, the elder called to the dead man, saying, 'Brother, where have you put your master's pledge?' And he answered back and said, 'I have hidden it in my house, under the leg of the bed.' And the father said to him, 'Rest again until the last day.' And when the brothers saw it they feared and fell at his feet. And the elder said to them, 'This has not happened because of me, for I am nothing. But God has done it because of the widow and her children. For this is what is important (τὸ μέγα); God wants a soul not to have sin. And whatever one asks (εἴ τι ἂν αἰτήσηται) he will receive. So go and tell the widow where the pledge is.' And she took it and gave it to her master, and he did not take them as slaves. And all who heard of it glorified God."

18. The Lapsed Bishop

Yet another (πάλιν ἄλλος) elder, who had been a bishop in the city of Oxyrhynchus, told this story (he told it as if it were someone else's, but it was he himself who had done it). "I once decided (ἔδοξέ μοι)," he said, "to go into the desert, to see if I could find some faithful servant of God. So taking a few loaves of bread and water for about (ὡς) three days, I set out. And after three days the water ran out, and I did not know what I should do. And so, putting my faith (πιστεύσας) in the Lord, I commended myself into his hand and travelled three more days (ἄλλας τρεῖς ἡμέρας) without drinking water. And finally (λοιπόν) my body could no longer endure the labor of the road and I fell to the ground and slept. Then a man came and placed his hand on my mouth, and immediately I found strength such as though I had not travelled at all. And so when I saw that this power had filled me, I stood up and continued on through the desert. And after four more days my water ran out again, and I stretched out my hands toward heaven. And behold, the same man who had given me strength before again placed his hand on my mouth. And after seventeen days, I came upon (εὑρίσκω) a house and a tree and water and a man standing by them. The hair of his head was his clothing (for he was naked); it was all white. And when he saw me, he stood still (ἔστη) in prayer. And when he had finished the 'amen', he knew that I was a man and not a demon. And so taking hold (κρατήσας) of my hand, he asked saying, "How did you come here? And is everything in the world still well (ἔτι καλῶς ἔχει), and are the persecutions still happening (ἔτι εἰσίν)?" And I said, "I am travelling through this desert for the sake of you who worship God with truth. The time of persecution (τὸ δὲ τοῦ διωγμοῦ) is no more, by the grace of Christ. But tell me you yourself (αὐτός) how you came here." And he began to weep, saying, "I was a bishop, and when the persecution arose (γενομένου) I fell into great sin, and my faith was lost. For I could no longer bear the torture and denied Christ and sacrificed to Caesar. But when I returned to my senses (ἐν ἐμαυτῷ ἐγενόμην) I realized my sin and gave myself up to die in this desert. And I have been living here for forty nine years, and weeping and beseeching God that my sins might be forgiven. And the Lord gave me life from the fruit of this tree. But I had no confidence (πίστιν) that my sins had been forgiven until after forty eight years. I have only a few days ago been reassured (παρεκλήθην)." And when he had said that, he immediately got up and went away to pray for many hours. And when he had finished the 'amen', he came back to me. And when I beheld his face, I was afraid, for it had become like fire. And he said to me, "Fear not. For the Lord has sent you to bury my body." And when he finished speaking, he immediately stretched out his hands and feet and gave up his spirit. And so I took off (θείς) my garment, keeping one part for myself and casting the other part over his holy body, I laid him in the earth. And when I had buried him, the house immediately collapsed, and the tree was no longer to be found. And I wept greatly, beseeching God to give me the fruit of the tree, that I should remain in that place for the rest of my life (ὅσον χρόνον ἔτι ζῶ). But when that did not happen, I said to myself that it must not be the will of God. And so after praying, I went back to the world. And behold, the man who had first laid his hand on my mouth came to me again and gave me strength. And thus I went to the brothers and told them about that elder, and exhorted them to have faith (πιστεύειν) and to find God by abiding in the truth.

19. Cyril of Alexandria and the Heretic

Abba Daniel told of another great elder, who dwelt
(καθημένου) in Lower Egypt, who claimed (ἔλεγεν)
that Melchizedek is the Son of God. This father was
misguided (ἐπλανήθη) in this, but in other regards
(ὡς πρὸς τὰ ἄλλα) he was a faithful and righteous
man. The blessed Cyril, Bishop of Alexandria, heard
about him and sent for him to come. Now, he knew
that the elder was a man of God, and whatever he
would ask (εἴ τι αἰτεῖ) of God, he would reveal to
him. And because the father was only deceived in
this, but otherwise was sound (καλῶς ἔχων), Cyril
used this trick (σοφίᾳ), saying, "Abba, I beg you, for I
have two thoughts; the one tells me, "Melchizedek is
the Son of God," while the other says, "No, he is only
(οὐ, ἀλλά) a man and high priest of God." But since
I do not know what the truth is, I sent to you that
you might ask of God, for him to give you revelation
(ἀποκαλύψῃ) concerning this." The elder had faith
that God would answer him and said with confidence,
"Give me three days, and I will ask God concerning this, and will tell you who he is." So he went and
asked God concerning this matter (ῥήματος). And
coming back after three days, he said to the blessed
Cyril, "Melchizedek is a man." And the Bishop said to
him, "How do you know, Abba?" And he said, "God
revealed to me all the patriarchs, each of them coming up before me, from Adam to Melchizedek, and be
sure (γίνωσκε) that it is so." And so he went away and
he himself (καὶ αὐτός) also preached that Melchizedek is a man. And the blessed Cyril rejoiced greatly.

20. Honest Abba John

One of the fathers said about Abba John the Persian
that he was a righteous man and most faithful. He
lived in Arabia in Egypt. Once, he borrowed a silver
coin from a brother, and bought flax to do his hand-
iwork. And a brother came asking him and saying,
"Abba, give me a little flax, so that I can make myself a
garment." And he gave it to him with joy. And another came imploring him, "Give me a little flax, so that
I can make myself a garment." And he gave it to him
as well. And when other asked, he gave to all with joy.
And then the owner (κύριος) of the coin came and re-
quested it (θέλων αὐτό). And the elder said to him, "I
will go and bring it to you." And since he had nothing
to give back, he got up and went to Abba Jacob. For
he wanted to request him to give him another coin, so
that he could pay back (ἀποδώσῃ) the brother. And as
he was going, he found a coin on the ground, but he
did not take it. Instead, he prayed and returned to his
house. And the brother came again and pestered him
(κόπους αὐτῷ παρέχων) about the coin, saying, "Pay
back what you owe." And the elder said to him, "Give
me a little time and I will pay it all back." And he went
away again, and saw the coin on the ground where
it had been before. And praying again, he returned
home (εἰς τὰ ἴδια). And behold, the brother came
again pestering him. And he told the elder, "Bring it
now!" And so he got up again, and went back to that
place. And he found the coin there in the road. And
having prayed, he took it. And he went to Abba Jacob
and said to him, "Abba, when I was coming to you I

found this coin on the road. Sir, announce it to the rest of the brothers, in case (μή τις) someone has lost it. And if its owner should be found, give it to him." And so the elder went away, and for three days he announced it. And no one was found who had lost the coin. Then the elder said to Abba Jacob, "If then no one has lost it, give it to this brother; for I owe him, and I found it when I was coming to borrow a coin from you to pay back what I owe." And the father was amazed how he was in debt (ὀφείλων) and when he found it he had not taken it immediately and given it to him. For such a heart of truth did Abba John the Persian have, that if anyone came to borrow from him, he did not give it to him himself, but said to the brother, "Go and get yourself whatever you need (εἴ τινος χρείαν ἔχεις)." And if someone gave it back, he said to him, "Put it back in its place." And if the one who had taken never paid him back, he never said anything to him.

21. The Greedy Worldling

There was once a young brother who had an elder whom he loved (πρεσβύτερον εἶχεν ἠγαπημένον). And after a long time the brother came to him and the elder said to him, "What have you been doing this whole time (τοσοῦτον χρόνον), my child?" And he said, "I was in the city, father, on urgent business (διά τινα χρείαν)." So the elder said to him, "And what good thing did you hear or see there?" The brother said, "Not much good, but rather (εἰ μή) only hypocrisy. Yet I was amazed at one thing. For I saw that men who live in the city despise money even more than we who live here in solitude (κατ᾽ ἰδίαν)." The elder said, "How? Tell me this story." So the brother answered, "I saw two rich men, and one said, 'You owe me this much money, and here I have a book in which is written that your father owed this much on credit (δι᾽ ἐπαγγελίας).' And the other one said, 'No, my father already repaid the debt without writing it down, but trusting in your righteousness. The credit has been satisfied (πεπλήρωται).' And when they could not convince each other, they decided (ἔδοξεν αὐτοῖς) to swear an oath. And so the alleged (λεγόμενος) debtor said, 'If I swear that the debt has already been paid by my father, and do not give the money myself, I will seem to people to be a greedy man. Rather let us do this instead (μᾶλλον οὕτως γενέσθω ἡμῖν); either I will swear that the debt has been paid and will give it to you again a second time, or you swear to me that I still owe it to you, and do not take anything else (μηδὲν πλεῖον) from me, and do not come looking for the money." And all who heard it were amazed at the man's great wisdom." And so the elder said, "And you are right (ἔδει) to be amazed, my child, because you are young. But I will teach you, and you will find that it was nothing great, but everything was only hypocrisy." The brother said, "How, father, if he despised that much money, so that he might not appear to people to be a greedy man?" The elder said, "The one who despises money should also make every effort (πᾶν ποιεῖν) to save the soul of his brother. So if that man knew that his father had already paid back the debt, then why did he still say that he should swear an oath and pay it back again? What else (τί ἕτερον) was he doing but showing that his brother is evil and greedy before God and men? And he was showing that he himself is quite wealthy (πλουσιώτατος) and does not even need the money. This is not faith and wisdom, but hypocrisy. For his heart wants the money and glory with men, and his eye is evil." The brother said, "So what should he have done? The other man asked him to swear an oath." The elder answered, "If he was righteous, he would neither have sworn nor asked the other man to swear, especially (μάλιστα) since he was rich and knew that he had already paid the debt." The brother said, "He should not have paid the money a second time, though (οὐκ οὖν)?" The father said, "And is it not better for him to suffer loss and not swear, but gain love as well? And will he not receive all these things from the hand of God in the kingdom of heaven? So he should not have exposed (δεῖξαι) the man who was requiring the money from him as evil to the rest of the people by his hypocrisy.

For this man does not love his brother. So you see, my child, that God desires only these deeds: those that are done with a good will and a spirit of love for God." And the brother went away rejoicing.

22. Two Elders Quarrel

Two elders had been living together for a long time, and they had never had a quarrel (μάχη). The one said to the other, "Why don't we have a quarrel like other people." The other answered and said, "I don't even know how to quarrel (πῶς γίνεται μάχη)." The other said to him, "Here, I will put a stone in the middle and say, 'It is mine,' and you say, 'No, it is mine,' and that is how we will begin." So they put a stone in the middle, and one said, "It is mine." And the other said, "No, it is mine." And the other one said, "If it is yours, take it and go." And they left, not having found anything to quarrel over with one another.

23. The Devil's Bags

Abba Macarius once had his home in the desert; he
lived there alone, and not far away there lived more
brothers all together in another desert. Now, the elder
was watching the road. And he saw Satan travelling
down it in the body of a man. He was wearing a large
garment and had many bags in his hands. And the
great elder said to him, "Where are you going?" And
he said to him, "I am going to remind the brothers."
And the elder said, "And why do you have all these
bags?" And he said, "I am carrying these to give the
brothers something to eat." And the elder said, "All
of them (καὶ ταῦτας πάσας)?" He replied, "That is so.
If someone does not like one, I bring another. And if
he does not like that one either, I give him another.
He is certain to like at least one of them." And having
said this, he left. The elder remained watching the
road until he returned again. And when the elder saw
him, he said, "Hello (χαῖρε)." And he replied, "What
do I have to rejoice (χαίρειν) over?" The elder said,
"Why?" He said, "Because all of them have become
my enemies, and no one listens to me." The father
said to him, "Do you not have any servant there?"
And he replied, "I only have one servant there, and at
least he obeys (πείθεται) and does my will. And when
he sees me, he turns like the wind." So the father said
to him, "And what is this brother's name?" He said,
"Theopemptus." And after saying that, he left. And
Abba Macarius arose and went down to the brothers. And when the brothers heard about it, they took
palm branches and went out to meet him. And each

of them opened his home to him, thinking that the elder would stay with him. But he asked (ἐζήτει) who was the one called Theopemptus. And when he found him, he stayed with him. Theopemptus received him with joy. But in private, the elder said to him, "How are things with you (πῶς τὰ κατὰ σέ), brother?" And he said, "If you are praying for me, they are well." The elder said, "Are the demons not tempting you?" He said, "By the grace of God, I am well (καλῶς ἔχω)." For he was afraid to speak. The father said to him, "Behold, I have been living alone in the desert for a long time, and I am beloved by all, and the spirit of fornication still tempts me, an elder." Theopemptus answered and said, "Be sure (γίνωσκε), Abba, that it tempts me as well." The elder mentioned (εἶπεν αὐτῷ) other spirits to him as well, in order to get him to tell the truth (ποιήσῃ αὐτὸν εἰπεῖν τὴν ἀλήθειαν). Then he said to him, "How do you fast?" And he said to him, "Until the third hour." And the father said to him, "Instead (μᾶλλον), fast until night, and pray. And keep in your heart the words of the Gospel and the other Scriptures. And if an evil spirit comes to you, do not look to the earth, but always towards heaven. And the Lord will be with you at once." And so, having given the brother these words and prayed over him, the elder left for his own place. And when he was watching the road again, he saw that same demon walking by and said to him, "Where are you going this time (πάλιν)?" And he said, "To remind the brothers." And he left. And when he was coming back again, the holy man said to him, "How are the brothers doing?" And he said, "Badly (κακῶς)." And

the elder said, "Why?" And he said, "They are all my
enemies, and the worst thing (τὸ μεῖζον κακόν) is that
the one servant I had who used to listen to me, even
he is lost—I do not know how. Not even he obeys
me, but has become the worst enemy (ἐχθρώτερος)
to me of all. And I said I would not go there again for
a long time (εἰ μὴ μετὰ χρόνον πολύν)." And having
said that, he went away, leaving the elder, and the holy
man went into his house.

24. The Council of Satan

One of the elders living in the Thebaid said, "I was the
child of one of the Greek prophets, who worshiped
demons. Now, when I was a young child, I would sit
every day (καθ᾽ ἡμέραν) and watch my father enter
into the temple to make sacrifices to the demons.
One time I secretly went in after him to see what
would happen. And I saw Satan and his whole horde
of demons standing before my father. And behold,
one of Satan's princes (ἄρχων τις) came and bowed
(προσεκύνει) before him. And the Devil answered
and said to him, 'Where are you coming from?' And
he said, 'I was on the earth, and I caused (ἐποίησα)
wars and shed much blood, and I have come to give
you a report.' And he said to him, 'In how much time
did you do this?' And he said, 'In thirty days.' And
he gave orders for the prince to be whipped and said,
'That was all you did in that much time?' And be-

hold, another evil spirit knelt before him, and Satan said to him, 'And where are you coming from?' And the demon answered and said, 'I was in the sea, and I caused winds and destroyed ships and killed many people, and I have come to give you a report.' And he said to him, 'In how much time did you do this?' The demon said, 'In twenty days.' And he said that he should be whipped as well, saying, 'Why did you only do this in so many days?' And behold, a third came and knelt before him. And he said to it as well, 'And where are you coming from?' And the demon replied and said, 'There was a wedding in this city, and I caused a war and shed much blood and killed the groom and the bride, and I have come to give you a report.' And he said, 'In how many days did you do this?' And he said, 'Ten.' And he said for him to be whipped also for wasting (ἀπολέσαντα) so much time. And last of all, another came and knelt before him. He said, 'And where are you coming from?' And he said, "I have been in the desert for forty years now (ἰδοὺ τεσσαράκοντα ἔτη) with one man of God, and this night the elder fell into sin with a woman.' And hearing this, he stood up, embraced him, took of his own crown and placed it on his head and sat him on his throne, saying, 'Because you were able to do this great deed.'" And the elder said, "When I saw this, I said, 'What a mighty people (μέγα ἔθνος) the desert fathers must be.' And after God desired to save my soul, I went out into the desert so that I too might become as they."

25. Good Will

One of the fathers said, "If you do not first hate, then you cannot love. If you hate sin, you do righteousness, as it is written: *Depart from evil and do good* (Ps 34:14). But in all these things, the will is what God requires (τὸ ζητούμενον). For Adam did not keep the commandment of God, even though he was still in Eden (καὶ ἐν τῇ Ἐδὲμ ὤν). And Job maintained (ἐτήρησε) his righteousness, even though he was given over into the hand of Satan and sat on the ground crying out. So the will is the only good that God requires of man, and that he fear him at all times."

26. Short Sayings

An elder said, "If you live here by yourself, do not say in your heart, 'I am doing such a great work.' But rather consider yourself (ἔχε σεαυτόν) like a dog that men have thrown out of their presence (ἀπὸ προσώπου αὐτῶν) and keep outside the house, because it was bad and bit them."

27. The Contest

A brother living in Monidii would often fall into for-nication. And yet (καί) he did not give up, but prayed frequently and called on God all the more, weeping and saying, "Lord, whether I want it (κἂν θέλω) or I do not want it, save me. For I am evil and cannot forsake fornication, but you are God and can keep me from this sin. For if you have mercy on the just man, it is no great thing (οὐδὲν μέγα). And if you save the good man, who will wonder? For it is good to have mercy on the good. But have mercy on me, Lord, a sinner, that I might behold your love. For *the helpless commits himself to You* (Ps 104:14)." And he would say this every day (καθ᾽ ἡμέραν), whether he fell or did not fall. And once when he fell into fornication at night, he would stand up immediately and begin to pray. And the Devil wondered at his hope and confi-dence before God, and came up before him, saying, "When you pray, how are you not utterly ashamed to stand before God and call on his name?" And the brother said to him, "This place is an arena, and we are fighting with each other. Sometimes you are giv-ing and I am receiving, and other times I am giving and you are receiving. But know that I will be fight-ing you until death or until the last day comes. And I testify to you—for my Lord came to save *sinners to repentance* (Luke 5:32)—that I will not stop praying against you to God, until you stop fighting me. And let us see who will take the victor's crown (στέφανον), you or God." And when the demon heard this he said, "Indeed (ἐπ᾽ ἀληθείας), I will not fight with you any

longer, lest you receive a crown for your faith." And
the demon left him and released him from that day
forth. Behold, what a good thing hope is, and not
to give in but have confidence before God, even if it
happens that we must fight in the arena and fall often
into sins. And when the brother came to repentance,
he sat weeping over his sins. And when his soul said,
"You do well to weep," he said to his soul, "Why (τί)
do you call this doing well? For what does God want,
that one should lose his soul and sit weeping for it?
No, I want my soul to be saved."

28. Do Not Judge

There was a great elder who lived in the mountains of Syria. He had a brother who was quick to judge when he saw someone doing wrong. So often the elder would often exhort him about this, saying, "You are much deceived, my child, and only losing your own soul. *For what man knows the things of a man except the spirit of the man which is in him?* (1 Cor 2:11) And many often do many evils before men, and by themselves in secret they repent to God. We see the sin, but only God knows the good that they do. For many have lived their whole lives in evil and often have found repentance at death and been saved. Some men (εἰσὶ ἄνθρωποι) have also have many sins, who have been accepted because holy men have prayed for them. And so even if a man sees it with his very own eyes, let him not judge his brother. For there is one Judge, the Son of God. Every man who judges anyone makes himself an antichrist. For by becoming judge, he has taken the glory and the authority which the Father has given him."

29. *Woe to That Sinner*

The great John of Saba said, "Once when I was living in the desert, a certain brother came to me. I asked him how the fathers were doing, and he said to me, 'If you are praying for them, they are well.' And I asked him about a certain evil brother who had a bad reputation (ὄνομα). And he said to me, 'Be assured, father, that that evil man is still the same.' And when I heard this, I said, 'Woe to that sinner.' And when I said 'woe', I was carried away at once in a vision and saw myself standing before Golgotha. And behold, our Lord Jesus Christ was between the two robbers on the cross. And so I got up and approached to bow down, and I fell on my face at his feet. But when he saw this, he called to his holy angels with a loud voice, saying, 'Cast him out, for he is an antichrist to me. For before I could judge, he had already judged his brother.' And when I heard that I was afraid, and immediately fled from his presence. But the angels followed after me and took my garment and cast me out. And immediately I came to myself and said to the other brother, 'This is an evil day for me.' And he said to me, 'Why, father?' And I told him my vision and said, 'My garment is a sign from the Lord that I am a man of God. And behold, he has taken it from me and cast me out.' And from that day, I spent seven years wandering in the desert. I neither ate bread, nor did I enter into a house, nor did I see any man. And after that long time, the Lord again appeared to me on the cross as he had before. And he let his angels give me back my garment.' And when we heard the blessed John say that, we said, '*If the righteous one is scarcely saved, where will the ungodly and the sinner appear?* (1 Pet 4:18)'"

30. *Abba Macarius and Wine*

They said of Abba Macarius that when he was with brothers he set himself this rule (νόμον): "If there is wine, then drink for the sake of the brothers. And for one cup of wine, do not drink water for one day." The brothers did not know what he was doing, and gave him many cups. And the elder took them gladly, so that his flesh might not rejoice. But his disciple knew what was happening and said to the brothers, "May it not be (μὴ γένοιτο), brothers, do not give him any more! Otherwise, he will kill himself in his house by not drinking water." And when the brothers heard it, they did not give him any more.

31. *Go and Revile the Dead*

A brother came to Abba Macarius the Egyptian and
said to him, "Abba, tell me a word; how can I be
saved?" And the elder said, "Go to the tombs and re-
vile the dead." So the brother went, reviled them and
threw stones at them. Then he came and told the elder what he had done. And he said to him, "They said
nothing to you?" And he said, "No." The elder said to
him, "Go back (πάλιν) and bless them." So the brother
went and blessed them, saying, "Apostles, saints, and
righteous men." And he came to the elder and said to
him, "I have blessed them." And he said to him, "They
did not answer you?" And the brother said, "No." The
elder said, "You know how you reviled them and they
did not answer you? And how you blessed them and
they said nothing to you? In the same way you also,
if you want to be saved, become a dead man. Do not
care about the injustice of men, nor about their glory,
just as the dead do not care about these things. And
in this way you can be saved."

32. My Sins Fall to the Ground

A certain brother once fell into sin in Scetis. And when a council was called to judge what they should do to him, they sent to Abba Moses. But he refused (οὐκ ἤθελεν) to come. So the elders sent again to him saying, "Come, the people are waiting for you." So he arose and went. And taking a basket, he poured (ἔβαλεν) water into it and brought it to the council—and as he walked, the water spilled back out of the basket and fell to the ground. And the brothers came out to him and said to him, "What is this, father?" The elder said to them, "Look (ἰδού), my many sins fall to the ground behind me, and I do not see them. And now I have come to judge the sins of my brother." And when they heard this, they said nothing to the brother, but released him.

Core Vocabulary

The following list includes the 294 core vocabulary words utilized in this Greek reader. It is arranged alphabetically, and includes frequency of use in the New Testament.

Part of Speech	Word	Gloss	Frequency
(adj)	ἀγαθός, -ή, -όν	good	131
(verb)	ἀγαπάω	I love	147
(noun)	ἀγάπη, -ης, ἡ	love	116
(adj)	ἀγαπητός, -ή, -όν	beloved	61
(noun)	ἄγγελος, -ου, ὁ	an angel	175
(adj)	ἅγιος, -α, -ον	holy; saint (noun)	233
(verb)	ἄγω	I lead	69
(noun)	ἀδελφός, -οῦ, ὁ	brother	343
(noun)	αἷμα, -τος, τό	blood	97
(verb)	αἴρω	I pick up	101
(verb)	αἰτέω	I ask	70
(noun)	αἰών, -ῶνος, ὁ	an age	122
(adj)	αἰώνιος, -ον	eternal	73
(verb)	ἀκολουθέω	I follow	90
(verb)	ἀκούω	I hear, listen	428
(noun)	ἀλήθεια, -ας, ἡ	truth	109
(conj)	ἀλλά	but, rather; then (in questions); now (in commands)	638

(pron)	ἀλλήλων, -ους, -ους	each other, one another	100
(adj)	ἄλλος, -η, -ο	other, another	155
(noun)	ἁμαρτία, -ας, ἡ	a sin, sin	173
(part)	ἀμήν	verily, truly, amen	129
(part)	ἄν	untranslatable particle - makes a statement contingent	166
(verb)	ἀναβαίνω	I go up	82
(noun)	ἀνήρ, ἀνδρός, ὁ	man, husband	216
(noun)	ἄνθρωπος, -ου, ὁ	a human being; man	550
(verb)	ἀνίστημι	I cause to arise, arise	110
(verb)	ἀνοίγω	I open	79
(verb)	ἀπέρχομαι	I depart, go away	117
(prep)	ἀπό	from (gen)	646
(verb)	ἀποθνήσκω	I die	111
(verb)	ἀποκρίνομαι	I answer	231
(verb)	ἀποκτείνω	I kill	74
(verb)	ἀπόλλυμι	I lose; to perish (mid)	90
(verb)	ἀπολύω	I release	66

(verb)	ἀποστέλλω	I send	132
(noun)	ἀπόστολος, -ου, ὁ	an Apostle	80
(noun)	ἄρτος, -ου, ὁ	bread, a loaf	97
(noun)	ἀρχή, -ῆς, ἡ	a beginning	55
(noun)	ἀρχιερεύς, -έως, ὁ	chief priest, high priest	122
(verb)	ἄρχω	I rule; to begin (mid)	86
(verb)	ἀσπάζομαι	I greet	59
(pron)	αὐτός, -ή, -ό	himself, herself, itself (emph); he, she, it; the same	5645
(verb)	ἀφίημι	I let go; permit; forgive	143
(verb)	βάλλω	I throw; put; pour (liquids)	122
(verb)	βαπτίζω	I baptize	77
(noun)	βασιλεία, -ας, ἡ	a kingdom	162
(noun)	βασιλεύς, -έως, ὁ	a king	115
(verb)	βλέπω	I see	136
(part)	γάρ	for, since	1039
(verb)	γεννάω	I give birth; beget	97

(noun)	γῆ, γῆς, ἡ	the earth, land, ground	254
(verb)	γίνομαι	I become; am	669
(verb)	γινώσκω	I know, come to know; realize, recognize	242
(noun)	γλῶσσα, -ης, ἡ	a tongue, language	50
(noun)	γραμματεύς, -έως, ὁ	a scribe	63
(noun)	γραφή, -ῆς, ἡ	a writing, Scripture	50
(verb)	γράφω	I write	191
(noun)	γυνή, -αικός, ἡ	woman, wife	215
(noun)	δαιμόνιον, -ου, τό	a demon	63
(conj)	δέ	but, and (often untranslated)	2792
(verb)	δεῖ	it is necessary; must (impers)	101
(adj)	δεξιός, -ά, -όν	right; right hand (fem noun)	54
(adj)	δεύτερος, -α, -ον	second	51
(verb)	δέχομαι	I receive	56
(prep)	διά	through (gen); on account of (acc)	667

(noun)	διδάσκαλος, -ου, ὁ	a teacher	59
(verb)	διδάσκω	I teach	97
(verb)	δίδωμι	I give	417
(adj)	δίκαιος, -α, -ον	right, just, righteous	79
(noun)	δικαιοσύνη, -ης, ἡ	righteousness	92
(conj)	διό	therefore, for this reason	53
(verb)	δοκέω	I think; seem, decide (im-pers)	62
(noun)	δόξα, -ης, ἡ	glory	166
(verb)	δοξάζω	I glorify	61
(noun)	δοῦλος, -η, -ον	a slave	126
(verb)	δύναμαι	I am able, can	210
(noun)	δύναμις, -εως, ἡ	power, strength	119
(adj)	δύο	two	135
(adj)	δώδεκα	twelve	75
(conj)	ἐάν	if (subj)	333
(pron)	ἑαυτοῦ, -ῆς, -οῦ	himself, her-self, itself (refl)	319
(verb)	ἐγείρω	I raise up, arise	144
(pron)	ἐγώ	I	2584

(noun)	ἔθνος, -ους, τό	a nation; Gentiles (plural)	162
(conj)	εἰ	if (indic)	502
(verb)	εἰμί	I am	2462
(noun)	εἰρήνη, -ης, ἡ	peace	92
(prep)	εἰς	into (acc)	1767
(adj)	εἷς, μία, ἕν	one	353
(verb)	εἰσέρχομαι	I go or come in or into, enter	194
(conj)	εἴτε	if, whether	65
(prep)	ἐκ, ἐξ	out of, from (gen)	914
(adj)	ἕκαστος, -η, -ον	each	82
(verb)	ἐκβάλλω	I cast out	81
(adv)	ἐκεῖ	there	95
(pron)	ἐκεῖνος, -η, -ο	that	243
(noun)	ἐκκλησία, -ας, ἡ	assembly, congregation, church	114
(noun)	ἐλπίς, -ίδος, ἡ	hope	53
(adj)	ἐμός, -ή, -όν	my, mine	74
(prep)	ἐν	in (dat)	2752
(noun)	ἐντολή, -ῆς, ἡ	a command, commandment	67

(prep)	ἐνώπιον	in front of (gen)	94
(verb)	ἐξέρχομαι	I go or come out	218
(noun)	ἐξουσία, -ας, ἡ	authority	102
(adv)	ἔξω	outside	63
(noun)	ἐπαγγελία, -ας, ἡ	a promise	52
(verb)	ἐπερωτάω	I ask, question, demand of	56
(prep)	ἐπί	over, on, at the time of (gen); on the basis of, at (dat); onto (acc)	890
(adj)	ἑπτά	seven	88
(noun)	ἔργον, -ου, τό	work, deed	169
(verb)	ἔρχομαι	I come, go	634
(verb)	ἐρωτάω	I ask, question, demand of	63
(verb)	ἐσθίω	I eat	157
(adj)	ἔσχατος, -η, -ον	last	54
(adj)	ἕτερος, -α, -ον	other, another (of two)	98
(adv)	ἔτι	still, yet, even	93

(verb)	εὐαγγελίζω	I bring good news, preach the Gospel	54
(noun)	εὐαγγέλιον, -ου, -ν	good news, the Gospel	76
(adv)	εὐθύς, -εῖα, -ύ	straightway, immediately; straight (adj)	59
(verb)	εὑρίσκω	I find	176
(verb)	ἔχω	I have, hold	708
(prep)	ἕως	until; as far as (gen)	160
(verb)	ζάω	I live	140
(verb)	ζητέω	I look for, seek	117
(noun)	ζωή, -ῆς, ἡ	life	135
(conj)	ἤ	or	343
(adv)	ἤδη	already	61
(noun)	ἡμέρα, -ας, ἡ	a day	389
(noun)	θάλασσα, -ης, ἡ	the sea	91
(noun)	θάνατος, -ου, ὁ	death	120
(noun)	θέλημα, -τος, τό	will	62
(verb)	θέλω	I want, desire	208
(noun)	θεός, -οῦ, ὁ	a god, God	1317
(verb)	θεωρέω	I look at, behold	64

(noun)	θρόνος, -ου, ὁ	a throne	62
(adj)	ἴδιος, -α, -ον	one's own	114
(part)	ἰδού	behold! look!	200
(noun)	ἱερόν, -οῦ, τό	a temple	72
(noun)	ἱμάτιον, -ου, τό	a garment	60
(conj)	ἵνα	in order that, so that	663
(verb)	ἵστημι	I cause to stand, stand	155
(verb)	κάθημαι	I sit	91
(conj)	καθώς	as, just like, even as	182
(conj)	καί	and, even, also	9158
(noun)	καιρός, -οῦ, ὁ	time, an appointed time	85
(adj)	κακός, -ή, -όν	bad, evil	63
(verb)	καλέω	I call, name; invite	148
(adj)	καλός, -ή, -όν	good, beautiful	102
(noun)	καρδία, -ας, ἡ	the heart	156
(noun)	καρπός, -οῦ, ὁ	fruit	66

(prep)	κατά	down from, against (gen); according to, throughout (acc)	473
(verb)	καταβαίνω	I go down	81
(noun)	κεφαλή, -ῆς, ἡ	head	75
(verb)	κηρύσσω	I proclaim, preach	61
(noun)	κόσμος, -ου, ὁ	the world	186
(verb)	κράζω	I cry out	55
(verb)	κρίνω	I judge, decide	118
(noun)	κύριος, -ου, ὁ	the Lord, master, owner	717
(verb)	λαλέω	I talk, speak	296
(verb)	λαμβάνω	I take, receive	258
(noun)	λαός, -οῦ, ὁ	a people	142
(verb)	λέγω	I say, speak	2357
(noun)	λίθος, -ου, ὁ	a stone	59
(noun)	λόγος, -ου, ὁ	speech, thought, word, story	330
(adj)	λοιπός, -ή, -όν	remaining; the rest (noun); from now on, finally (adv)	67

(noun)	μαθητής, -οῦ, ὁ	a disciple	261
(adv)	μᾶλλον	more, rather	81
(verb)	μαρτυρέω	I bear witness, testify	78
(adj)	μέγας, μεγάλη, μέγα	large, great	245
(verb)	μέλλω	I am about to	109
(part)	μέν	on the one hand, indeed (often un-translated)	179
(verb)	μένω	I remain; live; wait	120
(adj)	μέσος, -η, -ον	middle, in the midst	62
(prep)	μετά	with (gen); after (acc)	469
(part)	μή	not, lest	1042
(part)	μηδέ	but not, nor, not even	56
(pron)	μηδείς, μηδεμία, μηδέν	no one (subj, impv)	91
(noun)	μήτηρ, -τρος, ἡ	a mother	83
(adv)	μόνος, -η, -ον	alone, only	117
(adj)	νεκρός, -ά, -όν	dead	130

(noun)	νόμος, -ου, ὁ	a law, the Law	194
(adv)	νῦν	now	147
(noun)	νύξ, -νυκτός, ἡ	night	61
(art)	ὁ, ἡ, τό	the	19889
(noun)	ὁδός, -οῦ, ἡ	a way, road, journey	101
(verb)	οἶδα	I know	324
(noun)	οἰκία, -ας, ἡ	a house	93
(noun)	οἶκος, -ου, ὁ	a home, house	114
(adj)	ὀλίγος, -η, -ον	little, few	52
(adj)	ὅλος, -η, -ον	whole, all	109
(noun)	ὄνομα, -τος, τό	a name	234
(conj)	ὅπου	where, where to	82
(conj)	ὅπως	how; so that, in order that	53
(verb)	ὁράω	I see	455
(noun)	ὄρος, -ους, τό	a mountain	63
(pron)	ὅς, ἥ, ὅ	who, which	1435
(pron)	ὅσος, -η, -ον	as much as, as many as	110
(pron)	ὅστις, ἥτις, ὅτι	whoever, whichever, whatever	144
(conj)	ὅταν	whenever	123

(conj)	ὅτε	when	103
(conj)	ὅτι	that, because, since	1296
(adv)	οὐ	not, no	1623
(conj)	οὐδέ	and not, not even, neither, nor	143
(pron)	οὐδείς, οὐδεμία, οὐδέν	no one, none, nothing, no (indic)	234
(conj)	οὖν	so, then, therefore	499
(noun)	οὐρανός, -οῦ, ὁ	the sky; heaven	273
(conj)	οὔτε	neither, nor	87
(pron)	οὗτος, αὕτη, τοῦτο	this; he, she, it	1403
(adv)	οὕτω, οὕτως	thus, like that	208
(adv)	οὐχί	not (emph)	54
(noun)	ὀφθαλμός, -οῦ, ὁ	an eye	100
(noun)	ὄχλος, -ου, ὁ	a crowd, multitude	175
(noun)	παιδίον, -ου, τό	a young child	52
(adv)	πάλιν	again, back	141

(prep)	παρά	from (gen); beside (dat); alongside (acc)	194
(verb)	παραδίδωμι	I hand over, betray	119
(verb)	παρακαλέω	I beg, exhort; comfort	109
(adj)	πᾶς, πᾶσα, πᾶν	all, every, each	1283
(noun)	πατήρ, πατρός, ὁ	father	413
(verb)	πείθω	I persuade; trust (perf); obey (pass, mid)	52
(verb)	πέμπω	I send	79
(prep)	περί	concerning, about (gen); around (acc)	333
(verb)	περιπατέω	I walk	95
(verb)	πίνω	I drink	73
(verb)	πίπτω	I fall	90
(verb)	πιστεύω	I have faith (in), believe	249
(noun)	πίστις, -εως, ἡ	faith, belief, trust	243
(adj)	πιστός, -ή, -όν	faithful, believing; reliable	67

(verb)	πληρόω	I fill, fulfill	86
(noun)	πλοῖον, -ου, τό	a boat	67
(noun)	πνεῦμα, -τος, τό	a spirit, the Spirit	381
(verb)	ποιέω	I do, make	572
(noun)	πόλις, -εως, ἡ	a city	163
(adj)	πολύς, πολλή, πολύ	much, many	418
(adj)	πονηρός, -ά, -όν	evil, wicked	88
(verb)	πορεύομαι	I go, travel	153
(noun)	πούς, ποδός, ὁ	a foot	93
(adj)	πρεσβύτερος, -α, -ον	elder	66
(prep)	πρός	to, towards (acc)	700
(verb)	προσέρχομαι	I come to	86
(verb)	προσεύχομαι	I pray	85
(verb)	προσκυνέω	I bow down, worship	60
(noun)	πρόσωπον, -ου, τό	Face; presence	78
(noun)	προφήτης, -ου, ὁ	a prophet	144
(adv)	πρῶτος, -η, -ον	first	159
(noun)	πῦρ, -ός, τό	fire	71

(adv)	πῶς	how?	103
(noun)	ῥῆμα, -τος, τό	a word; thing	68
(noun)	σάββατον, -ου, τό	the Sabbath	68
(noun)	σάρξ, σαρκός, ἡ	flesh	147
(noun)	σημεῖον, -ου, τό	a sign; miracle	77
(noun)	σοφία, -ας, ἡ	wisdom	51
(verb)	σπείρω	I sow	54
(noun)	στόμα, -τος, τό	a mouth	82
(pron)	σύ	you (sing)	2908
(prep)	σύν	with (dat)	128
(verb)	συνάγω	I gather to-gether	59
(noun)	συναγωγή, -ῆς, ἡ	a synagogue	56
(verb)	σῴζω	I save	108
(noun)	σῶμα, -τος, τό	a body	142
(conj)	τέ	both […] and […]	215
(noun)	τέκνον, -ου, τό	a child	101
(verb)	τηρέω	I keep, guard	70
(verb)	τίθημι	I put, place	100

(pron)	τίς, τί	who? which? what? why?	579
(pron)	τὶς, τὶ	someone, something, a certain one, a certain thing, anyone, anything	538
(adj)	τοιοῦτος, -αύτη, -οῦτον	such	57
(noun)	τόπος, -ου, ὁ	a place	94
(adv)	τότε	then, at that time	160
(adj)	τρεῖς, -τρία	three	69
(adj)	τρίτος, -η, -ον	third	62
(noun)	ὕδωρ, ὕδατος, τό	water	78
(noun)	υἱός, -οῦ, ὁ	son	377
(verb)	ὑπάγω	I go	79
(verb)	ὑπάρχω	I am	60
(prep)	ὑπέρ	on behalf of (gen); beyond (acc)	150
(prep)	ὑπό	by (gen); under (acc)	220
(verb)	φέρω	I carry, bring; endure	66
(verb)	φημί	I say	152

(verb)	φοβέομαι	I fear	95
(noun)	φωνή, -ῆς, ἡ	sound, voice	139
(noun)	φῶς, -φωτός, τό	light	73
(verb)	χαίρω	I rejoice	74
(noun)	χαρά, -ᾶς, ἡ	joy, delight	59
(noun)	χάρις, -ιτος, ἡ	grace	155
(noun)	χείρ, χειρός, ἡ	a hand	177
(noun)	χρόνος, -ου, ὁ	time	54
(noun)	ψυχή, -ῆς, ἡ	soul, life, one-self	103
(adv)	ὧδε	here, to here	61
(noun)	ὥρα, -ας, ἡ	an hour, time	106
(conj)	ὡς	as, like; approximately	504
(conj)	ὥστε	so that	83

www.ingramcontent.com/pod-product-compliance
Lightning Source LLC
Chambersburg PA
CBHW071012120626
46546CB00003B/1056